D1070924

THE NEW SOCIAL MARKETPLACE

Notes on Effecting Social Change
in America's Third Century

COMMUNICATION AND INFORMATION SCIENCE

A series of monographs,
treatises, and texts

Edited by
MELVIN J. VOIGT
University of California, San Diego

HEWITT D. CRANE • The New Social Marketplace: Notes on Effecting Social Change in America's Third Century

RHONDA J. CRANE • The Politics of International Standards: France and the Color TV War

GLEN FISHER • American Communication in a Global Society

JOHN S. LAWRENCE AND BERNARD M. TIMBERG • Fair Use and Free Inquiry: Copyright Law and the New Media

ROBERT G. MEADOW • Politics as Communication

VINCENT MOSCO • Broadcasting in the United States: Innovative Challenge and Organizational Control

KAARLE NORDENSTRENG AND HERBERT I. SCHILLER • National Sovereignty and International Communication: A Reader

In Preparation

JOHN J. GEYER • Reading as Information Processing

BRADLEY S. GREENBERG • Life on Television: Content Analysis of U.S. TV Drama

MICHEL GUITE • Telecommunications Policy: The Canadian Model

ITHIEL DE SOLA POOL • Retrospective Technology Assessment of the Telephone

CLAIRE K. SCHULTZ • Computer History and Information Access

THE NEW
SOCIAL MARKETPLACE

**Notes on Effecting Social Change
in America's Third Century**

HEWITT D. CRANE

Staff Scientist
SRI International

AUG 23 1982

ABLEX Publishing Corporation
Norwood, New Jersey 07648

For Russell, Douglas, and Daniel
and especially for Sue

Copyright © 1980 by Ablex Publishing Corporation.

Printed in the United States of America.
Library of Congress Cataloging in Publication Data

Crane, Hewitt D.
  The new social marketplace.

  (Communication and information science)
  Bibliography: p.
  Includes index.
  1. United States—Social conditions—1960-
  2. United States—Social policy.   3. Social action.   4. Social change.   I. Title.
II. Series.
HN65.C68   973.92   80-11674
ISBN 0-89391-063-5

ABLEX Publishing Corporation
355 Chestnut Street
Norwood, New Jersey 07648

CONTENTS

PREFACE

These notes evolved during the heat of the late 1960s and early 1970s, when disgust with the Vietnam War was mounting rapidly. The anti-war movement found strong leadership and support among the young of America's middle and upper classes — an unusual rebellion of the young of a society's "haves." Their rebellious feelings against "the establishment" were fueled by taking on the nation's Black cause at the same time. Racial strife and riots, especially in the larger cities, added further stress to a nation already strained by the problems of Vietnam. Out of this youthful problem-solving mood were born the environmental movement and with it efforts to stop development and "progress," at least of the more familiar sorts. Amid the social chaos of the times, many people — young and old — began "dropping out" of the system. Many young people even left the country to avoid the draft.

These notes were my friend during that period, easy to talk to early each morning, as I tried to sort out in my own mind what was really going on. Amid great flurries of social activity it is easy to be deceived by the trees and to miss the forest entirely. What seemed clear was that a new form of involvement and decision making was evolving in this country. No longer did we seem as trustful of government, industry, or our leaders. From now on, society was saying, we the people were going to have a more direct voice in social planning and decision making; and we have indeed seen a steady trend toward citizen involvement in policy making through initiative, referendum, and social action. We have voiced our concern over issues in such areas as the military, supersonic transports (SSTs), marijuana use, get-out-of-Vietnam, anti-ballistic missiles (ABMs), the use of nuclear power, and taxes; and we have campaigned to save the air, hills, rivers, bays, national parks, wildlife, and whales. It is likely that this march to the ballot of public opinion will continue in the near future.

However, it seemed equally clear that for a population to be able to trade easily and effectively in broad, complex social issues, new kinds of social organization would be required. A new kind of marketplace would be needed for handling what we might think of as social, in contrast to physical, goods and services.

Severe difficulties and pitfalls are inherent in postulating new institutional forms. However, instead of trying to justify and defend each proposition against every possible "reality" — "Exactly who will pay for it in the short run?" "Who will benefit?" "Who will lose?": difficult questions indeed — I am more concerned with sketching pictures of some future reality, with the hope that the pictures themselves will infiltrate and drift among the layers of social awareness and perhaps offer some guide to that ever-present army of innovators and entrepreneurs who are continually on the prowl for new ideas and opportunities.

Exploring the future is somewhat like playing football in grass eight feet tall. Every once in a while the players must jump high enough to see the goal posts and then settle down to a few small scrimmage plays. In developing the concepts described in this book, I have tried to jump high enough to perceive some distant goals as well as to outline some plays for immediate action that seem promising.

. . . .

The author wishes to acknowledge the contributions of Bill Linvill, John Sunderland, and Bob Glass in generating and sorting out some of these ideas, and of Shirley Hentzell, Charlotte Irvine, and Klaus Krause in helping to polish them.

INTRODUCTION

As our social concerns expand at a dizzying pace, we are faced with injunctions from all sides: "Decentralize government." "Solve the energy problem." "Protect our resources." "Get more involved." These voices at times seem more confusing than the problems themselves; our weary reply is "How?"

This book suggests that the answer to the question "How?" will be found in the evolution of social mechanisms for dealing effectively with complex, rapid change. On the level of society as a whole, dealing with the issues that confront us — such as energy, pollution, transportation, resources, welfare, warfare, and numerous others — will require the evolution of an extended marketplace for social goods and services similar to our present highly successful marketplace for physical goods and services. On the individual level, the accelerating pace of change will require the evolution and acceptance of a "recycling lifestyle," in which a person can change careers or lifestyles without penalty — even several times over a lifetime. As will be seen, the extended social marketplace is also a central element at this level. Building that marketplace is a major task and opportunity of America's third century.

A guiding image behind this notion is that the most serious problem we face is not the many issues *per se* that occupy the minds of planners and analysts and those generally bent toward such concerns, but the lack of processes for dealing effectively with the entire set — what in

Chapter 1 is called the "social curriculum." For as many groups that claim "A" is the solution to a given problem there are often as many others promoting "not A." These groups might be guided by different perceptions or be concerned about the effects that a "solution" in one area might have on certain other problem areas; other groups may be "one-issue" groups or be worried about different clusters of problems. Beyond conflicting views, many issues are so complex technically that it is often difficult to understand even the nature of the problems, much less the proposed solutions. Every one of us is a layman in the face of the complexity and the wide range of issues confronting us. A few of us know a great deal about certain aspects of certain issues, but no single individual and no single group has a firm grasp on even one whole problem. It is not possible, because all of our major issues are so highly interrelated. To cope with the interrelatedness is our *real* problem, and that is what an effective marketplace can achieve.

As understanding matures, perceptions change and often what once looked like a reasonable solution, even to experienced analysts and planners, may come to look ridiculous. We need, then, processes that can accommodate continual searching, communication, and feeling our way. Robert A. Solo put the difficulty this way:

> Mark it well, the communication of new ideas, new conceptions, new understandings, inventions, new ways of doing things, between individuals fixed in their ways and intent upon their separate objectives is difficult and rare. . . . In fact the problem is far more difficult, for the communication of invention is rarely from man to man, from inventor to innovator, from source to destination directly. Rather it is a transmission of an idea "through channels," infiltrating, drifting, passed along through layers upon layers of organization. Beyond the barriers that separate individual from individual, it must cross those which set apart groups and communities. (1967, p. 119)

It would be folly to claim that the American social marketplace referred to over and over again in this book is nonexistent. It exists, and it contains mechanisms and processes of social interaction that have matured and filtered down through two centuries of existence as a nation. What *is* claimed is that the marketplace currently lacks parts and pieces that are crucial for coping with today's problems: mechanisms to facilitate the continual infiltrating and drifting of new ideas along the layers upon layers of social organization. This book suggests some forms that such mechanisms might take, but first it is necessary to explore the more general features of the social marketplace.

THE SOCIAL MARKETPLACE

Physical goods—shirts, ties, shoes, luggage, automobiles, TVs—are developed and produced by manufacturers. Buyers examine, compare, and decide whether to buy a particular good depending, for example, on the urgency of need, their available capital, the reputation of the producer, and how the purchase of one good might influence or preclude the purchase of others. The procedures and structures that organize these activities constitute the physical goods and services marketplace.

Social goods are ideas. They may become formalized in judicial rulings or in new pieces of legislation, or they may remain informal social guidelines or unwritten laws. Social goods may also eventually evolve into physical goods, as the concept of nuclear power evolved into actual nuclear facilities. Like physical goods, social goods are shaped by their inventors and proponents and must eventually be sold and bought in the world of social commerce. Voters, communities, and fellow legislators (that is, buyers) examine the goods and select among them according to similar criteria—for example, need, reputation of the proponents, and the effects on resources.

Whereas the "bugs" in a physical design are generally worked out in private, the bugs in social goods must be worked out on the stage of social action, for there are no comparable social laboratories. The development and evolution of social goods, in other words, is served by a much more public research and development function. Furthermore, working out the details is not as simple as for physical goods because social requirements are much more difficult to understand and come to grips with, and social goods affect and interact with each other in much more complex ways than do physical goods. But both are similar in that new ideas for physical and social products are continually being developed, some of which have major impact, although most are simply refinements.

With the current mood in the United States, individuals and communities are no longer leaving the buying and selling, or even the creation and development, of social goods or ideas primarily to elected representatives or to industry. Individuals and a wide range of social-action groups are actively proposing and promoting their own ideas for new and improved kinds of products, social systems, and social regulation and legislation.

There is certainly nothing new about vigorous social action. What is new, perhaps, is the general mood of the country in trying to get into all conceivable issues — from nuclear energy and insecticides to restricting land development and saving endangered species of every sort. However, many of these issues are extremely complex, requiring — apart from faith and commitment to a cause — a great deal of knowledge and information. If social action is to be reasonably founded, and if society is to have a clear idea of the tradeoffs among competing ideas and the competing uses of limited resources, proposals must be based on solid information and informed insight. Uninformed or misinformed action groups can be as dangerous to society as a completely passive population. It is in this sense that we can think also of the need for a vastly extended marketplace for knowledge and information goods and services.

To set the scene another way, we can say that, until recently, our major social planning was based largely on a professional/client relationship, not unlike our relationship with a doctor or a lawyer. Our representatives and technical specialists in business and government were the presumed keepers of professional competence, and they "knew best"; we were the clients who lived with their decisions. We could afford such a laissez-faire attitude because our country was physically and psychologically immense, we seemed to have a large margin for error, and we were not too concerned with long-range consequences. Now, however, as our physical and psychological space seems increasingly cramped and issues come crashing into each other, the feeling is growing that we have less margin for error; and many have come to feel an urgent need to become more involved with making and selecting social policy.

The current era can be characterized as a shift, then, from a basically professional/client relationship to a more interactive marketplace relationship for social planning. We are witnessing the evolution of such a marketplace. On the "consuming" side are individual citizens, communities, and independent consumer, watchdog, and action groups; on the "producing" side are researchers, technologists, manufacturers, and policy makers from the public, private, and independent sectors. But the space between is a confusing, noisy, and disorganized arena, with few of the critical mechanisms necessary to allow a market system to operate smoothly and effectively.

This chaotic transitional stage reflects the fact that a marketplace relationship requires very different mechanisms than does a professional/client one. Whereas a professional/client relationship in social planning, as in a medical or legal case, requires a relatively simple exchange ("These are the problems"; "These are the available solutions"), or no exchange at all, a successful social marketplace will require—like our marketplace for physical goods and services—many levels of interconnection to facilitate effective dialog between "producers" and ultimate "consumers."

The recent drive for greater public involvement recognizes that social action is indeed open to everyone. For most of us, however, the notion of more involvement in an open marketplace is dismaying. "More involved? I'm already so overloaded that I can't conceive of another meeting," or "I can barely make it from morning till night now without exhaustion." Another typical response is "I've been involved and accomplished next to nothing."

What we need most of all at a personal level is a way to achieve greater involvement with *less* effort, not more. We also need to feel that involvement is likely to lead to positive effects. These goals are precisely what a higher level of organization—a marketplace—can achieve.

A marketplace brings together buyers and sellers, consumers and producers, bargain seekers and scoundrels. A viable marketplace has effective means of communication, brokerage, and policing services that facilitate the exchange of ideas, goods, and services. For example, to reach our present scope and efficiency in the production and distribution of physical goods—to the point where equitable distribution of work opportunity requires us to continually shorten the workweek and enforce earlier and earlier retirement—we had to evolve a highly intricate set of market mechanisms: capital formation; research, production, warehousing; wholesale and retail selling; national, regional, and local centers; brokerage, communication, and distribution systems; methods of policing and regulation; and skills in analysis and strategy. Our new marketplace will deal in different sorts of goods—social and knowledge goods—but will require the evolution of many of the same kinds of mechanisms.

These mechanisms will have to evolve at all levels: national, regional, and local. Many of our contemporary problems derive from the effects of technology, which lie far beyond the boundaries of any single city, county, or state; as a result, we have seen the development of an increasingly centralized industry and government that have become unwieldy and, in many ways, add to our long list of problems. If we are to cope with current issues, we will need new perspectives and public understanding, especially new skills, machinery, and institutions at the local and regional levels.

In short, the achievement of broadly based participation, invention, experimentation, and innovation will require much greater decentralization. Revenue sharing is a step in this direction, although cities tend to use such funds in tackling traditional problems of immediate concern rather than applying them to unfamiliar new problems of long-range importance. Without new machinery, the energy provided by such partial steps as revenue sharing cannot be applied in new ways.

Daniel Bell, who popularized the term "post-industrial society." suggests the following evolution of social systems:

> A pre-industrial society is a game against nature. . . . An industrial society is a game against fabricated nature, in which Man has used energy to make large machines that add to his power to transform his world. . . . The Man-machine relationship is a fairly recent phenomenon in terms of Man's history and Man's experience. But the Man-Man relationship [built on a broad base of rapidly accumulating information and knowledge] has never been the central issue in terms of his history or his attempts at survival. (1976, p. 47)

A new type of society is in order, then — an information society requiring new kinds of relationships among people. Our extended marketplace is aimed at providing the means for coping with these new kinds of relationships and institutional bases, just as our now familiar physical goods and services marketplace helped us into and through the industrial era.

From this time of intense social action might well evolve a science and theory of social goods and services. It will not be as easy as a science and theory for physical goods and services, however, for there is no comparably simple measure of performance. "Price" in social goods includes far more than dollars. But, however premature a theory may be at this time, it seems clear that we are entering a phase of new institution building, from which in fact new theories may evolve. A discussion of the kinds of institutions that may be useful and necessary for dealing more effectively with social goods and services makes up Part One of this book.

RECYCLING AND EDUCATION

Although much of the surface heat of the Vietnam era has disappeared, the feelings and behavior that characterized those times are important indicators of deep-rooted social problems. The press at that time, for instance, gave a great deal of attention to the seemingly large number of dropouts from among people of all ages and all walks of life — people disgusted with what was happening in Vietnam and in society in general, and who were seeking more meaningful roles and occupations than "simply chasing the almighty dollar." Also, with the inability of schools to cope with the children or the issues of the times, education was suddenly charged with being "irrelevant."

It was becoming clear that with rapid, complex social change, there is a fundamental need for individuals to be able to shift careers and lifestyles with much greater ease — in effect, to "recycle" themselves. A recycling mode would represent a much more flexible relationship between individuals and society than the one-career style to which we have been generally conditioned. In fact, a recycling mode and an extended social marketplace would be highly complementary. On the one hand, successful recycling requires that individuals be able to explore and understand the changing needs, issues, and opportunities in, society — requirements that could be met by an extended social marketplace; on the other, people in a recycling mode could represent an important input to a newly evolving social market system in which many new kinds of entrepreneurship and job opportunities will have to evolve. Finally, the demands of a recycling lifestyle, and of rapid social change in general, will require greater training and experience with both the exploratory and operational aspects of living and problem solving — requirements that could be aided by a more mature social marketplace and by some shifted emphasis in formal education. The ideas of a recycling society and of extended roles for public education are explored in Part Two of this book.

This book does not offer simple remedies or quick answers. Rather, it is a kind of handbook for the journey through the *terra incognita* of America's third century, with a hint of some of the frontiers that seem to be visible.

Part One
THE SOCIAL
MARKETPLACE

I

ELEMENTS AND PERSPECTIVES
OF AN EXTENDED SOCIAL MARKETPLACE

Social decision making and problem solving are weak to the degree that important elements are missing from the social marketplace. In this chapter, we discuss the need for organized knowledge goods and services, the need for facilitating the emergence and activities of a broad array of initiator groups and associations, and the need for social brokers who, as in any vital marketplace, help to organize and facilitate transactions. Realization of these needs will require extending the social marketplace by the evolution of new institutional forms.

We suggest also that a rapidly changing society can be thought of as passing through a social curriculum analogous to an academic curriculum. Long experience has shown that an academic curriculum can be considered as having two parts—content and process—and that if the academic processes are inadequate or inappropriate, content transfer may be weak. Similarly, although we are seemingly overcome by the content aspects of many social problems, it can be argued that we are suffering even more from the lack of social processes by which we can cope effectively with so much information. The processes of the social curriculum are yet another way to view the nature of the missing pieces of our social marketplace.

The U.S. marketplace for physical goods and services is highly intricate. None of us deals directly with RCA or with General Motors; between consumers and producers are many levels and kinds of activities that facilitate our transactions, as suggested in Figure 1. Through this mechanism, we deal easily with physical goods. We have access to highly evolved shopping areas and shopping centers; if these centers do not fill our needs, we can turn to intricately cross-referenced catalogs and directories that help us determine who makes what, at what price, and how we can obtain the goods we want. Often, there is a veritable army of agents, salespersons, and brokers to help us interpret, translate, and consummate these transactions. By and large, we exercise a certain amount of control over the production side of the system by what we buy or don't buy and from whom.

We can draw a similar picture for the production and consumption of social goods and services, except that our interconnecting system

PRODUCERS   CONSUMERS

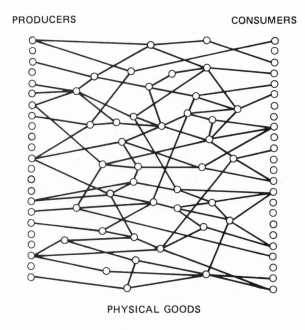

PHYSICAL GOODS

Figure 1   An intricate interconnection system between the producers and consumers of physical goods.

currently is sparse in relation to our needs; there is a relatively empty middle (see Figure 2). Although we are encouraged to take a more active part in resolving social issues and influencing legislation, we find that information and policy decisions evolve from remote places — government, industry, "think tanks" — that seem outside our grasp. The difficulty goes beyond a lack of proper access and organization, for substantive involvement also requires the availability and consumption of a great deal of complex information and knowledge.

The effects of an "empty middle" in our social marketplace can perhaps be appreciated in terms of our view of the Russian system, in which a relatively small clique of Kremlin planners presumably controls every level of production. Our magazines and journals have for decades carried jokes and cartoons on the confusion and injustices that result from such a top-down, centralized, "commissar" system of government control — in effect, the chaos of an empty middle in which the critical bargaining, feedback, and brokering components are missing. In contrast, we have pointed with pride to our own highly evolved, interactive, and efficient physical goods systems. Ironically, however, when it comes

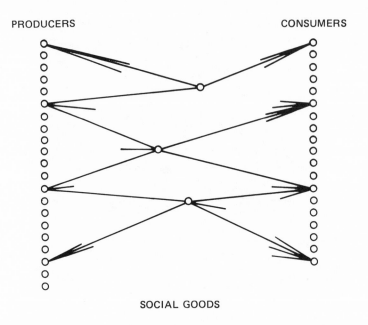

PRODUCERS

CONSUMERS

SOCIAL GOODS

Figure 2 The "empty middle" in the production and distribution system for social goods.

to social planning and knowledge goods and services, we are now easily subject to similar confusion (and jokes). Our technical information, expertise, and large-scale system planning derive from high-level planning agencies, from Washington, from universities and research institutes, and from industrial laboratories, but until recently there has been little opportunity for individual and community contribution, feedback, or control beyond the activities of the ever-present lobbyists and pressure groups who work behind the scenes.

A NEW CONTEXT FOR SOCIAL DECISION MAKING

Over the last several decades, we have seen the steady growth of a huge, highly centralized, and remote government. Control of technological development, through the evolution of large corporations, has similarly become centralized and remote. As a result, many people have lost hope of having the slightest impact on the shaping of modern society, and with it, all interest in personal participation. The society is so vast and its centers of big business and big government so remote that many of us feel we have no possible share in the control of the institutions that directly affect our lives. In this vastness, many of us also sense that we are losing the spirit of community and belonging that is so important to a satisfying life.

Although most of us still want our voices heard through the elective process, we have found that it is difficult to vote wisely, or that our votes do not of themselves offer opportunities specific enough or effective enough to influence the outcome of an issue about which we are personally concerned. To augment the elective process, we have evolved a rash of vocal and visible action-oriented groups to give further support to our concerns: groups to save our rivers and bays, civil rights groups, pro- and anti-population-control groups, pro- and anti-ABM groups, amnesty groups, gun control groups. What seems necessary is a sense of increased participation in strategizing and planning, both locally and nationally, in ways that will decrease our alienation and overcome the barriers born of technical specialization and complexity. We also need to find ways of coping with the dense interconnectedness of complex issues. In particular, we must be able to take into account simultaneously many complex issues if we are to avoid the unanticipated effects of isolated decisions.

We are heading into a period of intense social bargaining and challenge at all levels—local, regional, national, and international—and in a new context:

- *TV and Telstar awareness.* With modern communication, the haves and have-nots both here and abroad are now in a position to compare their lives and determine more specifically than ever their needs and wants and the means of obtaining them.
- *Greater individual and small-nation threat.* One person can hijack an airliner and hold a hundred hostages; a nuclear weapon in the hands of a country the size of New York's Central Park can kill as many people as it would if used by a major nation. Thus, we are called upon to develop a larger world view that encompasses more than a few superpowers.
- The finitude of the biosphere. The resources used and the waste products generated by one system substantially alter the opportunities and constraints in other systems. Fuel used by automobiles is not available for heating; water used for abstracting oil from shale is not available for agriculture. No problem lends itself to a single solution, and no solution is free from spiraling effects.

In the past, the private sector, through active competition, offered us multiple problem-solving approaches that served us well in developing and evolving efficient products and industrial techniques. Now, however, many of our important social needs derive from the *interaction* of major systems in society, and the burden of meeting these new needs appears to fall more and more on the public sector (government). As a result, we must now search out ways in which the public sector can facilitate social exploration with the variety that the private sector has offered in physical products and physical exploration.

THE ROLE OF THE PUBLIC

Crisis-oriented policy making seems almost endemic to democracies, perhaps because executive or legislative actions aimed at preventive measures generally lead to charges of do-gooding and meddling in free processes. Gas rationing, in 1973 and again in 1979, for example, is one such crisis decision that depended on recognition of an apparent energy shortage for public acceptance. However, our margins of tolerance for unanticipated effects grow smaller as our problems become more complex and more interrelated.

Indeed, our energy crisis need not have been a surprise. Through history up until 1960, the world had consumed five cubic miles of oil.[1] During the ten years from 1960 to 1970, the world consumed another five cubic miles. The current rate of world consumption (with the United States accounting for almost one-third) is nearing one cubic mile of oil per year! No genius was needed to see, even several decades ago, that changes would eventually have to be made in both acquisition and consumption patterns.

Given the complexity and interrelatedness of current issues, it is hardly reassuring to have our planning guided by elected officials, professional planners, and researchers who, regardless of their sincerity, find that reelection and follow-up funding are generally easier if they "play it safe." Also, centralized research, planning, and decision making — without the widespread involvement of society — can promote short-term perspective, short-term arrangements, and partial or isolated solutions. Professionals, whether in research or in government, become expert on what demands immediate attention, what is immediately attractive, or at least what is politically feasible. These short-term considerations do not necessarily match, and often contradict, the real needs of the nation.

The problem is that no one person can be expert in the full set of complex interactive issues that we face; there are experts on only small and isolated parts of the set. Expertise applied to any part of the problem set may plug a leak here or there, but isolated expertise has no special talents or knowledge for predicting where new leaks and unanticipated effects may appear. Greater participation by society in idea generation and the public business on a steady, long-term basis — instead of the current method in which problems suddenly explode into public consciousness — would help assure that the nation's real long-term needs are addressed. The question is how such participation can be achieved.

Broader involvement of people at all levels would also deter policy makers and researchers from relying too heavily on easily quantifiable analyses and from overlooking larger concerns. The analysis of the wrong issue or an incomplete set of issues to seemingly great numerical

[1]There are approximately 1 trillion gallons to a cubic mile.

accuracy can numb us into believing the real problem has been grasped, but in fact this emphasis often excludes the contribution of those who might have a deeper grasp of the fundamental issue. For instance, it is simple enough to count policemen, squad cars, uniforms, and small arms; it is much more difficult to evaluate and know how to cope with increasing lawlessness. It is simple enough to count doctors, nurses, hospital beds, and ambulances, but much more difficult to evaluate the state of health care delivery and to develop health systems that meet the needs of the widest range of people.

Broader public involvement could also give planners and elected officials the strength to pursue courses of action that are difficult, if not impossible, without broad-based constituency support. However, such involvement is hard to achieve because our society is not yet geared for it. The mechanisms for educating the public on complex issues and for facilitating effective exchange with technologists and policy makers are not yet well developed.

DEVELOPING A SOCIAL CURRICULUM PERSPECTIVE

We can use an academic curriculum analogy to help us appreciate the nature of the missing pieces — the empty middle — in our marketplace for social and knowledge goods and services. For example, we think of a school curriculum as a means of helping a child learn about society as well as how to develop his or her potential within the society. In the same manner, we can view ourselves as a society attempting to learn to cope simultaneously with a broad array of social topics. Our social curriculum involves a broad array of interrelated concerns or subjects: energy, land use, mass transportation, waste management, food, population, welfare, unemployment, crime, race relations, health care delivery, education systems, drug misuse, urban congestion, depletion of resources, the arms race, international relations, and many others. We can call these areas the *content* of our social curriculum.

Just as academic systems are often discussed in terms of "process" as separate from "content," so can we evaluate our social system on both levels. In academic terms, process refers to everything not directly related to content: how and where schools are built, transportation, free lunch programs, counseling, health services, how teachers are selected and motivated, how teachers motivate students, the extracurricular activities, and so on. From many decades of experience, we have learned that if any of these environmental or human processes are inadequate, transfer of content may be weak.

Currently we are suffering from a lack of social processes by which individuals, groups, and institutions can deal effectively with information and social issues: processes to help us grasp the different content areas of our social curriculum and processes to help us convey our ideas in the new marketplace.

A curriculum concept also helps to put into a more realistic light the actual form our involvement might take. In a university, every student takes only a tiny fraction of the courses available. Nonetheless, because a *comprehensive* system of information transfer exists, we have assurance that a full body of knowledge is being passed on to the benefit of society. So, too, any single individual, group, or institution can address only a tiny fraction of the social curriculum. But in a vital social marketplace, each one of us could be assured that, although our individual involvement was very limited, we are still part of a comprehensive system of social problem solving.

DISPENSING INFORMATION IN A SOCIAL MARKETPLACE

Statements claiming that Americans are the best-informed people in history are in themselves empty. Although we are perhaps better informed than ever, in our continually evolving technological society our information needs seem to grow faster than our sources develop. In addition, we face a problem of information dispersal; the vast amount of information on which we currently depend is not properly generated, distributed, or marketed to meet the needs of a technological, knowledge-based, highly mobile society in the process of rapid change. We are all—young and old, rich and poor, liberal and conservative—suffering from a new form of intellectual malnutrition: too much disorganized information and too little of the knowledge we need.

The complexity of our social issues and the rapid pace of social change require that we have the best possible access to relevant information. Our awareness of ecological problems has created a demand for new environmental information and well-trained specialists; an increasing problem with drugs has led to the development of systems of drug therapy, drug clinics, and halfway houses; increased international relations create a need for people who read and speak all the languages of the world; new opportunities with video recording and cable TV have created a need for additional information on mass communication forms and processes. Solving our problems helps to define our opportunities; they are opposite sides of the same coin.

The need for knowledge is thus twofold. To cope individually, everyone must have easy access to information. To cope as a society, we cannot leave society's problems entirely to the specialists, be they in government or in industry. In the future, then, we require not only an extended marketplace for social action but also an extended marketplace for knowledge and information. Without the mechanisms or processes of wide distribution of organized and relevant information, we will find it difficult to obtain the widespread participation in decision making that we seek. Without them, also, government and industry will become even more centralized and dominant.

SOCIAL PROBLEM SOLVING

To see how best to facilitate social problem solving, we need to dissect the problem-solving process itself. The solution to any problem, social or otherwise, passes through a number of phases: (1) identification of the problem, (2) initial exploration to determine the essence of the problem, (3) formulation of alternative procedures or solutions, (4) selection of one or more alternatives, (5) mustering necessary support, (6) implementation, (7) achieving a product, or result, and (8) evaluation. Evaluation might lead to a redefinition of the problem and the start of a new cycle.

Most of the serious problems facing society require many cycles of this problem-solving process since their large scope, great uncertainty, long gestation period, and interrelatedness cause many changes in their configuration.

Exploratory and Operational Modes

Figure 3 divides our eight problem-solving steps into two different modes: an *exploratory* mode, whose primary function is to illuminate an issue or problem; and an *operational* mode, whose primary function is to implement a solution. Whereas the exploratory phase is open ended and diffuse, the implementation phase is highly structured and direct. Implementation requires an established hierarchy of leader-

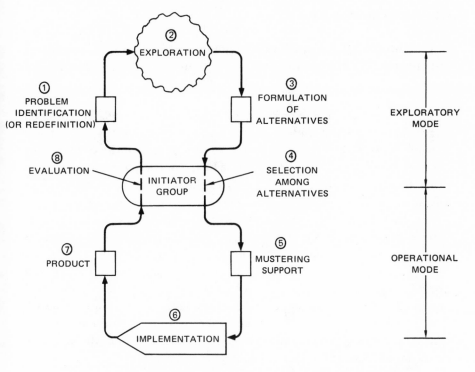

Figure 3　The exploratory and operational modes of the problem-solving process.

ship and responsibility with specific plans and fixed goals; it strives for efficiency through formal agreements and strict time frames for obtaining results. The no-nonsense, high-pressure aspects of the operational mode tend to inhibit the exploratory mode; similarly, the open-ended aspects of exploration inhibit efficient action. Accordingly, conceptual exploration is best removed from day-to-day operations.

Initiators

Efforts to solve a problem always begin with a concerned individual or group. The first major action of the group, called here an *initiator* group, is to explore the problem, possibly to the extent of organizing a special exploratory group, or consortium. The initiator might also assume responsibility for support of the exploration as well as for pursuit of alternatives and implementation. Thus, the initiator group is the basic link between the exploratory and operational modes and the responsible decision maker.

Improved social problem solving requires facilitating the evolution of effective initiator groups and associations in all sectors of society.

Brokers

Social change on any significant scale demands broad social agreement, and the underlying exploration and implementation will almost invariably demand an extensive broadening of the constituency concerned with an issue. To stimulate broad participation in a problem that has been identified and partly explored, the initiator will often need to operate as a broker or engage outside brokerage help.

Brokerage is fundamental to any marketplace. Except in the most trivial situations, brokers are needed to bring together buyers and sellers and, in complex situations, to expand the constituency of interest. To be effective, brokers must understand the needs and expectations of the participants and appreciate the relevant economic, political, and legal constraints. Our extended social marketplace will ultimately also require new forms of brokers — social brokers — who are familiar with the dynamics of large groups, who understand the issues, and who know the realities of local and regional problem solving.

DEVELOPING A NEW RELATIONSHIP AMONG THE SECTORS

The formation of an informed and effective populace would be facilitated not only by a network of informed social brokers and broker institutions but by a new kind of relationship among the major sectors of society.

The Public and Private Sectors

It is conventional to refer to government and private institutions as the *public* and *private sectors* of society. Individuals exercise a degree of control over these institutions, or sectors, through the ballot and the marketplace. Public institutions, in turn, exercise formal control over both individuals and private institutions through executive, legislative, and judicial actions. Private institutions control by influence; they attempt to guide public institutions by lobbying and individuals through advertising and public relations. Figure 4 is a highly simplified representation of these numerous interactions, with individuals and the public and private sectors making up the three points of a triangle.

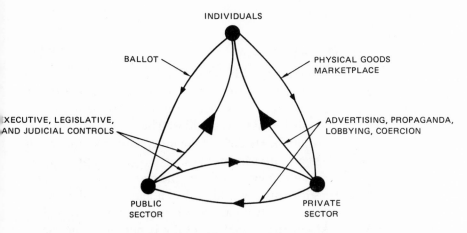

Figure 4 Interactions of individuals and the public and private sectors.

Early America was a society composed mainly of individuals and their small associations; the private sector was a highly decentralized system of small-scale entrepreneurs, and the national government was an almost invisible force in daily life. Modern America, standing now on a vast base of semiautonomous corporations and a very large government, is a much different society. From the perspective of individuals, the relative strengths of the controls in modern America are suggested by the sizes of the arrowheads in Figure 4. In particular, as a result of its importance in technological and industrial development, the private sector has gained immense power over us as individuals. It not only serves our physical needs, but it also creates and shapes these needs. Similarly, as the result of a long history of social invention and development — in particular since the New Deal, when government took on a strong role in human welfare — public institutions have also come to exercise strong influence over us. So much momentum has developed that the ballot and the marketplace — i.e., what we choose to buy — offer relatively weak forms of response and control.

Concentrating on each corner of the triangle, many people maintain that our current problems can be solved simply by the development of greater consciousness and social responsibility within private business, by a greater commitment by individuals to public service and the public interest, and by more resourceful, streamlined, effective governmental regulation. But merely reinforcing the corners of the triangle in this way is not enough — it doesn't alter the nature of the interactions.

The Independent Sector

R.C. Cornuelle, in his book *Reclaiming the American Dream,* suggests that incorporating the voluntary sector, or what he calls the "independent sector," of society into the substantive interactions of the day in a more intense way could well be the impetus we need for new structural evolution. He defines the independent sector as consisting of volunteer organizations, churches, action groups, professional societies, political organizations—in short, the traditional associations so prominent in American history. This independent sector plays an important part in evolving creative, participatory, and responsive societal problem solving. Although its goal generally is not profit but social value, the independent sector, like the other sectors, operates through a marketplace mechanism; and the strength of any organization depends on how many and how strong are the people who support its ideas and programs. Thus, we can expand the triangle diagram of Figure 4 to a pyramid, as illustrated in Figure 5.

In this nation's first century, the independent sector took on the major burden of individual and local problems, from care of the sick and underprivileged to education. But with growing population, advancing technology, massive industrialization, and the continually in-

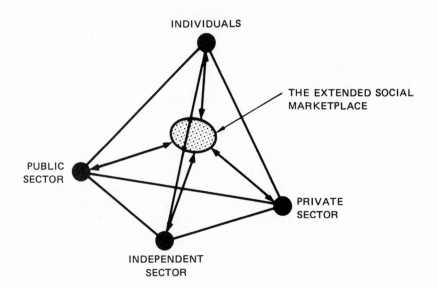

Figure 5 An extended marketplace to facilitate interactions among the sectors.

creasing scale of both public and commercial business, the independent sector has grown weak and disorganized (although, as Cornuelle [1965, p. 35] notes, "the sector's dimensions are fantastic, its raw strength awesome"), and it has been performing unreliably.

> [It] uses men and material badly. It doesn't signal needs properly. It doesn't fill shortages automatically. . . . Its agencies penalize fraud, but not incompetence. . . . (p. 50)

> The commercial sector spends millions looking for new markets, getting ready for new demands. The government sector spends millions looking for new items of public business. The independent sector spends next to nothing. Yet of the three, it knows least about its own strength and how and where and when to put it to work. . . . There are millions of people longing to be called to service [but with the state of disorganization of the independent sector] . . . there is no longer much they can do. (pp. 96-98)

Under the pressures of unrest, confusion, and the desire for greater participation, the independent sector — through different forms of citizen action groups — is again more visible and is showing new vitality. The current era of vigorous independent action dates from such individuals and groups as Saul Alinsky, Ralph Nader, Martin Luther King, Common Cause, the antiwar groups, women's liberation, and population and ecology groups.[2] In effect, a large range of action groups is forming to match a vast range of social issues. With respect to what we have been calling social goods, the current period is a bit like early America, with its highly decentralized marketplace for the production of physical goods. That early piece of American history is generally viewed as a highly innovative and productive period, where the experimental and inventive skills of many individuals found effective outlet in a highly decentralized market system. A decentralized marketplace for social goods and ideas might well lead us into another highly creative period of our history.

An informed and revitalized independent sector can serve as the social subconscious, monitoring the public and private sectors, which act as the operational units of society. The monitoring function is vital

---

[2]An Environmental Protection Agency brochure entitled "Don't Leave It All to the Experts" has this to say of independent sector involvement in environmental issues:

> Organized citizen groups are the mechanisms through which public opinion is best applied to environmental decision making. They magnify and concentrate the views of like-minded individuals. They give new meaning to the concept of participatory democracy. (p.3)

because the operational sectors have evolved highly structured patterns that tend to be applied over and over: It is easy to design one more freeway. This accumulated experience leads to great efficiency, but it also inhibits change in basic patterns. Because it has no operational responsibilities and because its constituent associations can form and reform as needed, the independent sector can exert a formidable assortment of pressures to secure change. Pressures exerted by the independent sector derive from the deep feelings and perceptions of many individuals alone and in concert; they can serve to continually readjust societal patterns in accord with the needs of the total social organism.

Without broad-based pressure, it is too easy for the public and private sectors, relying heavily on expertise, to develop programs that ignore needs that are inconvenient or costly, don't fit into classical analyses, or are not perceived. An expert can suggest what *can* be done in a given situation, at least from his own limited perspective, but it takes all of us to decide what *should* or *should not* be done. Although expertise can readily develop cost-benefit analyses of alternatives for us to accept or reject as a society, that still leaves us with a type of shopping list approach. If we want specialists to reflect our needs more directly, society must enter earlier into the definition of the problems and the development of alternatives.

Merely including the independent sector is still not enough, however. Revitalizing the independent sector and resynthesizing all sectors requires new means by which individuals and representatives of the public, private, and independent institutions can effectively meet to explore problems together — the extended social marketplace suggested in Figure 5.

FACILITATING GROUP ACTION

There seems to be a tendency for people to associate in groups, based on style of thinking, the nature of experience, or the desire for certain forms of action. Facilitating this tendency through the guaranteed right of assembly has probably been the hallmark of the great American experiment. The oft-quoted Frenchman Alexis de Tocqueville, writing in the early 1800s, emphasized the importance of this "characteristically American tendency" to form groups and associations.[3]

_____

[3]The two chapters entitled "Political Associations" and "Public Associations" offer a perspective worth rereading in light of current problems.

There is only one country on the face of the earth where the citizens enjoy unlimited freedom of association for political purposes. This same country is the only one in the world where the continual exercise of the right of association has been introduced into civil life, and where all the advantages that civilization can confer are procured by means of it. . . . (1965, p. 385)

Americans of all ages, all conditions, and all dispositions, constantly form civil associations. They have not only commercial and manufacturing companies, in which all take part, but associations of a thousand different kinds — religious, moral, serious, futile, extensive or restricted, enormous or diminutive. The Americans make associations to give entertainments, to found establishments for education, to build inns, to construct churches, to diffuse books, to send missionaries to the antipodes; and in this manner they found hospitals, prisons, and schools. (p. 376)

Thus it is by the enjoyment of a dangerous freedom [the right of unlimited political assembly] that the Americans learn the art of rendering the dangers of freedom less formidable. (p. 390)

These myriad civil associations, according to de Tocqueville, convey enormous power to the people that can counteract any overweening power of government.

The tendency to form associations is still strong among us. The legal right of association, however, is no longer sufficient as we strike out into our third century. Effective group action today requires ready access to large amounts of data and background information as well as the moral authority conveyed by the right of assembly.

To try to halt the construction of a nuclear power plant requires not so much blind faith or religious zeal as real information on its dangers, benefits, and unanticipated effects. Actions based purely on emotion without effective information can be as socially destructive and frustrating as action based on narrow expertise. An antidote to emotionally dominated action, to narrow expertise, and to top-down government is to facilitate the formation of informed associations and consortia within the public, private, and independent sectors of society. That is one way in which we can build on tradition and evolve more effective problem-solving processes for the benefit of society. Effective social-action associations can make visible the varied concerns of different groups and constituencies, initiate and coordinate social action, facilitate the division of labor, free other constituencies to tackle additional problems, and create a sense of productive participation in government and society.

We have learned that good intentions and sentiment alone don't erase poverty, racial injustice, hunger, or war. We need skills, effective strategies, new metaphors to see by, tenacity, and, most of all, a way of bringing all this together. Subsequent chapters will explore the kinds of institutions that might serve as underpinnings for the extended marketplace that can perform this organizational task.

II

EXTENDING THE NETWORK:
MEDIA-KNOWLEDGE CENTERS

In developing the social marketplace, the most powerful tool we can put into the hands of the public is good access to information and education. Currently, we have an impressive array of adult and continuing education courses in subjects ranging from electronics and computer programming to ecology and transcendental meditation. But the schoolroom alone has never generated a complete education. We have always been dependent on libraries, bookstores, newspapers, travel, friends, relatives, and experience to assist in the learning process. Now we need a new kind of activity to augment our more formal education—what we call here a media-knowledge center—to help us reach a higher level of capability in using our knowledge resources.

A media-knowledge center can be a focus for a wide and varied arsenal of information. Shopping centers are an example of a local synthesis of resources already developed in our physical goods marketplace. We now need a similar synthesis for social and information resources. Many of the elements of such a center already exist; we must simply bring them together in a new combination.

Ultimately, the development of a successful social marketplace will require the evolution and operation of organizations and institutions dealing in social goods on the local, regional, national, and even international levels. Of these, the most numerous and most fundamental will be the local institutions, which will be the most immediately accessible to individual citizens. One possible form of such an institution—conceived of here as the media-knowledge center—is considered in some detail in this chapter, followed by the higher-level institutions in succeeding chapters.

A VISIT TO A MEDIA-KNOWLEDGE CENTER

Let us look forward several decades into our third century—the clothes look a little different, but we don't yet need the help of science fiction to understand how things work. We are going over to the local media-knowledge center, a trip of about 15 miles.

This is the children's first visit, and their initial impression is one of disappointment—it looks like any other shopping center, except that nobody sells everyday merchandise. Their interest quickly awakes when they discover that the center has booked a small traveling show that has to do with nuclear power plants. They play with the exhibits for a while, getting a charge out of pushing the button that controls the emergency shutdown procedure at the first sign of reactor instability.

We came to do an errand, so we pull the children away from the exhibits and go into the travel agent's office to arrange for a vacation. This year, it's either Australia or Egypt, but which? The agent will not charge us for making reservations and arranging either trip, but there is a small consulting fee.

The agent suggests places and activities we might enjoy in both countries and calls an information store across the mall for some videotapes so that we can see for ourselves. We walk a couple of doors down to a set of viewing cubicles where we stick a coin in a slot to pay our "rent" on the tapes. Based on our impressions of the two countries, especially information on our special interest, home architecture, we make our reservations for the Middle East.

We also want to rent videorecords for our home videorecord player, so we head over to the information store. Here, the kids are fascinated by the computer-controlled printer, which is feeding out two chapters of a 30-year-old treatise on the Vietnam War for a history student, then provides that day's *Manchester Guardian* editorial for a local newswriter, and then the text of the Idaho law on nuclear energy for a panelist at the traveling show. It turns out that the store has a whole set of videotapes and videorecords on the area we are going to visit, so we rent some to further prepare for our trip.

It is lunchtime, so we go to the restaurant, stopping for a moment to take a look at the hostel where a group of bicyclists from France are checking in. After lunch, we drop in at the cable TV studios and look through the glass windows. In one studio, a journalism class is taping some interviews with a group of Arabian students who have been staying at the hostel. In another studio, a large one, a public hearing is going on about the need to extend the airfield runway over a public highway.

Past the cable TV studios are meeting rooms housing seminars on nuclear energy. Farther on is a repair center for videotape players, hi-fi equipment, videocameras, copy machines, and printers. Next comes a place the children have been waiting to visit: the computer network center.

The children have already prepared questions they want to ask the center's computer, and they present them to the programmer. The programmer checks the questions to make sure they are asked in a form the computer can answer and then takes our credit card and sticks it in the slot. Jeff has learned to use the terminal at his school and wants to put in his own question. He sits down at the keyboard and types slowly, until the question is perfect on the TV screen above. He waits until the computer is free; when the green light flashes, he pushes the button and runs over to the printer to wait for the slip with his answer. As we are about to leave, an aide comes in from the public hearing with a set of questions to be fed into the computer before the afternoon session. The programmer sits down and begins to work.

The art store, which is on the way to the transit terminal, is already crowded with school children, some of them renting master-teacher lessons on videotape to take down to the music practice rooms, some renting music-and-light films to take to the dance rooms. We stop a few minutes to watch a drama troupe perform on the small stage outside the coffeehouse.

Beyond, on either side of the entrance to the transit station, are two large units. One is an employment agency; in its display window a huge map of the world keeps lighting up in different patterns of dots. Adrienne wants to know what it is, so we go in. The woman behind the job location counter explains to Adrienne that she puts a magnetically coded application form into the slot, and the map will light up in every city that has a suitable job. She points out the green dots — job locations that match an applicant's current skills and for which relocation costs would be paid. More exploratory positions — such as working at an antropological dig or counting gray whales — show on the map as orange lights; study fellowships are represented by yellow lights.

The employment counselor gives Adrienne a sample printout to take home with her, and we decide to explore the shop front on the other side of the transit terminal. This office is still known as "the unemployment office," despite its official sign saying "Department of Human Resources." Through this central location, the basic services available at local offices are supplemented by a wide range of specialized services: special education for the handicapped, rehabilitation, relocation grants, and certification for people who have learned a new skill.

We leave because we have to get home, but we anticipate numerous returns as the children proceed through their schooling.

GATHERING THE EXISTING PARTS

By moving out a few decades to the media-knowledge center, we recognize that most of the parts already exist, though some of them are in only embryonic form. We don't know their joint value because we see them only separately and in the context of our present daily routines; the elements currently are scattered in typical shopping areas, dependent only on business considerations and not on their potential relationships to each other.

We currently have chains of bookstores and chains of record and tape stores, but we don't yet have a comprehensive information store that organizes the sale or rental of slides, tapes, books and movies. Our public libraries are moving in this direction but have the resources to serve only a small number of people within the boundaries of a particular community (and they rely on scarce public funds); universities offer similar services but limit their clientele to students and faculty and aren't really set up to serve the greater community.

We are envisioning, then, a larger grouping that can be self-supporting and that is accessible to the largest possible segment of the population. The logical core of this grouping is a cluster of media goods and services that can attract a large clientele and serve important education functions. From this core, we can expand the center to encompass public services geared toward meeting social needs in an organized fashion.

Meeting Our Information Needs

Grouping media and knowledge outlets would create the potential for sharing common facilities and prorating the cost of specialists and equipment over a broad base. Even more to the point, the close proximity and the rich, multidimensional access would allow a person to find out in one visit what was available in any and all media forms. If his interest were trade with North Africa, and if inventories were merged across media boundaries, he could gain access in all media forms to information on North African tariff regulations, culture, or current insights with a single query. The merging, in turn, would provide motivation for generating new material to fill observed gaps in the multimedia inventory.

The role of providing information about the goods in today's bookstores has fallen more and more to people who are removed from the store's customers — manufacturers' representatives and commercial advertisers; clerks seldom do more than maintain the inventory and ring up the sales record. Private bookstores are inhibited from providing full-time resource people, such as those now used in libraries, because the expense is prohibitive and the emphasis now is on bookstores as mere purchase points. But a larger resource base could be justified in a media-knowledge center in which resource people, extra equipment, and pooled revenue offer a potential profit for customers as well as shop owners. This approach to inventory maintenance and consumer access can, of course, be applied equally to audiovisual material, computer services, and copying equipment designed for printing information on demand. An intercenter exchange network, like the current interlibrary loan system, would further increase the skills and scope of any given center and decrease the need for any one unit to support unwieldy overhead costs. A cluster of audiovisual facilities could serve an additional consumer need through their ability to create intense and realistic environments useful for learning about other areas, new careers, and social issues, as well as for general entertainment.

Nor should we overlook the travel agent, who, although connected to an extremely efficient reservation system, now has little direct connection to the educational or informational aspects of travel. For a business, vacation, or exploratory trip there is often value in seeing what it looks like beyond the edge of the travel folder or to have leads to interesting side trips. These additional services would be made possible if travel agents were an integral part of a media-knowledge center.

We have also seen in our sample center that business could be concentrated in a way that justifies skilled maintenance and repair. Eventually, grouping together the maintenance and repair services for movie and slide projectors, tape players, video equipment, a multi-theater configuration, private projection booths, computer equipment, a cable-TV origination system, as well as special equipment for demand printing, would provide a large enough base to justify high-level maintenance and repair skills at the local levels in addition to regional and national levels convenient to manufacturers.

Facilitating Community Outreach

It is easier to foresee the media elements of a local center than the wider-range elements that relate more directly to social issues. But a broad grouping of media-knowledge goods and services could certainly serve as the core of a more extended center. Let us consider some of the likely public and private components that might be stimulated by such a core.

Public Service Facilities. Every community has a large array of interconnected public service programs: health and welfare, employment, social security, special education programs, legal aid, and others. However, these services overlap considerably, making it difficult for agencies to find their constituents or for individuals to find their way through the maze of agencies. Public service agencies are deliberately duplicated and scattered to provide easy access to clients. However, if representatives from each agency were located in the same place, consumers would have a clearer view of the available services, find it more convenient to make preliminary inquiries, and be able to decide more readily which ones are most appropriate for their needs. To date, public agencies have evolved very much as a seller's market in that it is difficult for consumers to know whether they have alternatives and, if so, which services to select. A media-knowledge center could provide important one-stop access to community resources that would be a convenience to the agencies as well as their constituents, since agency workers could obtain additional services from the core units to help in the performance of outreach tasks.

Private and Independent Groups. A media-knowledge center could conceivably encompass a range of tenant representatives and small offices from the private and independent sectors of society as well. A power and light company might want to display its new model of a nonpolluting generating station. An ecology or campaign organization might want exhibit space and a place to sign up new adherents. Professional societies, industrial groups, unions, foundations, and proprietary educational and information service groups would also benefit from clustering representatives at a center of sufficient scale. Built around a highly efficient core of media and knowledge services, these groups could share not only a common space but also many common services, substantially improving their own efficiency.

Educational Campaigns. A media-knowledge center would be a natural setting for developing focus on local and regional issues. The occupants of the center could concentrate their displays, shows, and stocks periodically on a particular subject, somewhat as present shopping centers have Easter sales or Thanksgiving promotions, but emphasizing an *idea* rather than commerce. Energy conservation or mass transit displays and shows could be assembled at a center much as museums presently create their exhibits—partly internally created and partly supplemented by elements from other museums (or centers). These promotions would bring new people into the centers. They would also increase experimental sharing among regions, as each center borrowed relevant materials and displays from other centers. If many of the occupants of the center became involved in such shows, contributing their particular insights and information, the combination of focus and information would provide another quantum jump in our understanding of the social issues with which we have to deal.

GETTING STARTED

As in any evolving organism, it is impossible for any one part or element to mature fully alone; an advance in one part generates growth in the others. Thus, the existence of even embryonic regional centers (see Chapter III) or traveling shows (see Chapter IV) would develop a demand for enhanced local capabilities to complete the skeleton of a social network.

To build a new and extensive center of the form we have described and have it open three months from now would be like trying to go from no flight at all to international jets in a single step. New institutions and new capabilities evolve gradually; some Americans still have never been in an airplane, others have never used a telephone, and many still do not see how a computer could help them. But at some point in our third century, highly aggregated centers of the sort we envision will exist, and we will use them in many more ways than are proposed here.

Creating a new kind of center means searching out those elements that are already operational and finding a way to bring them together into a new synthesis. The airplane was the stimulus for bringing together gasoline stations, machine shops, merchandise stores, telephone lines, travel agents, roads, and car rentals into a new synthesis in a remote location. But just as the flight of Wilbur and Orville Wright had in it no hint of the airline stewardess, the flying doctor service, fire fighting, cloud seeding, or airborne fertilization, traffic control, and stocking of lakes, it is difficult to foresee all the new social capabilities that a core of media-knowledge services might eventually facilitate.

Achieving sufficient scope, flexibility, and competence in media-knowledge centers requires some minimum size. "Local" centers might eventually grow to serve as much as a congressional district (although political connection is not intended in this image of size), resulting in a network of some 500 such centers across the country. A district-wide center — with proper support — could gather and organize massive amounts of material and make the information available to the more local bookstores, audiovisual shops, and libraries.

Initial entrepreneurship is logically the responsibility of the private sector, although a point may be reached where local centers are so important to society that universal access is necessary and subsidies seem in order. (As centers evolve, the private sector might continue to operate the core facilities, while more and more of the peripheral activities become publicly supported.)

As a way to start, a consortium of groups or companies that has experience at the software, hardware, and communications levels could explore the possibilities and effect of a coalition among chains of bookstores, record shops, theaters, and travel agencies at the retail level; book publishers, experimental theater and video groups, more formal movie and video film makers, and educational companies at the software level; and electronics and audiovisual equipment manufacturers at the hardware level, perhaps with the addition of cable-TV franchisers. An enlarged grouping might first be profitable only in more affluent areas of concentrated population, but the potential for a viable private sector venture exists.

Like a shopping center, airport, flea market, or movie house, a well-designed media-knowledge center could serve as an interesting place for the whole family to go on a Sunday afternoon, after dinner, or — in sparsely populated areas — for an overnight holiday. Even more important than a place to go, a network of such centers, of different sizes and scopes, would represent an important piece and level in the evolving social marketplace. It would allow us to function at a new level, valuable to society and to ourselves. It would allow people who get engaged in issues important to them greater access to information, it would help to widen the participating fraction of society, and it would reduce the general feeling of futility and remoteness.

III

BUILDING REGIONAL ORGANIZATION: EXPLORATION-BROKERAGE CENTERS

Because the issues of the social curriculum transcend the boundaries of local jurisdictions, institutions analogous to the local media-knowledge centers are also needed at the regional and national levels. The initial function of regional exploration-brokerage centers would be to broaden the education of specialists who would become the "professors" of the social curriculum. Eventually they would also assume a brokerage function, coordinating the dissemination of information, obtaining cooperation among interest groups, and promoting constituency building for wider public and institutional involvement in various issues. At the national level, centers concerned with specific subjects of the social curriculum would serve as brokers and coordinators for the regional centers, as information resources and as clearinghouses for ongoing experiments.

Regional exploration-brokerage centers could be modeled, at least initially, after existing academic centers, but their concerns would be much more externally oriented. Participation would be based not on academic credentials but on involvement with regional problem solving. The basic process would be one of mutual education among researchers, specialists, planners, policy makers, legislators, and others. As active participants in their communities, the centers could also provide resource people for schools, develop educational materials, offer student internships, and form links among groups concerned with regional issues.

The solution to any problem requires a level of readiness and organization consonant with the level of the problem. It is clear that many current problems have distinct geographical and regional clusterings that do not fit within the decision-making and implementation units that now exist. To achieve economies of scale and responsiveness to geographical differences, we are likely to need a broad network of centers. Figure 6 shows a highly simplified diagram of such a network. In this scheme, national centers address specific social functions such as communication, transportation, energy, health care, and housing—the subjects of the social curriculum. Many national centers currently exist; but without other kinds of centers to facilitate more local involvement and feedback, national centers can offer only downward-directed inputs, and half of the two-way process is missing.

A logical synthesis would be one in which activities for each major social function are coordinated by a national center, which serves as a broker among regional centers, acts as a national exploratory center, and is a coordinator and clearinghouse for actual ongoing experiments. Each region in turn would bargain for funds on the basis of its own needs. Regional centers would use national funds, together with region-

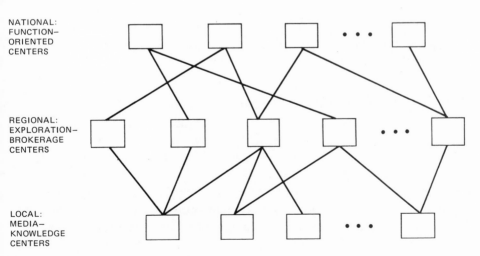

Figure 6 A system of national, regional, and local centers.

al and local funds, to provide brokerage for broad participation in regional exploration and experimentation. The third broad component of the network would be local centers, like the media-knowledge centers described in the preceding chapter, which would take the social problem-solving process one step farther, extending information and regionally developed expertise to the general public.

REGIONAL CENTERS: THEIR SCOPE AND RATIONALE

Our social problems vary from region to region: for instance, housing problems are not the same everywhere; the requirements of health-care delivery in the Los Angeles basin are very different from those in rural Appalachia. Although we recognize such variations among regions, regional organization is inadequately developed. Currently, planners or researchers who may wish to explore weather modification, for example, must consult separately with agronomists, biologists, meteorologists, economists, lawyers, and other specialists and then attempt to put the pieces together, usually without sufficient expertise. A regional center designed for the pooling of specialized knowledge could offer broad-based analysis of a cloud-seeding contract offered to a given county, for instance, or of a complaint issued by a state whose crops were adversely affected by a neighbor state's program (or lack of one).

A regional center designed to meet problems related to the region might serve a single metropolitan area, a portion of a state, an entire state, or several states, forming part of a network of perhaps some 50 to 100 regional centers throughout the United States.

Education of Specialists

How are we to develop the specialists who understand the details and the interactions among the many issues we will be exploring in our lifetimes—the "professors" of the social curriculum? We have few such specialists today, for it is only within the last several decades that most of us have begun to appreciate the complexity of the decisions we are facing. No university gives overview courses that teach how to pull together disparate problems, although interdisciplinary programs are a step in this direction. No federal agency has the answers. Ultimately, we can develop our social problem-solving skills only by working together cooperatively. Initially, the people of specialized expertise will need to learn from each other in order to broaden their base of skills. It is this pressing educational need which would first be served by the regional exploration-brokerage centers. Centers that serve initially as classrooms for these specialists would in turn serve an important operational role in societal planning and decision making.

The education of specialists to achieve broad-based expertise in many areas must proceed initially with specialists teaching each other. This type of education is happening now, although in an ad hoc and inefficient fashion. It is nothing new that highly motivated individuals seek out others and form alliances; but the process would be enhanced enormously with more formal support and organization so that it does not entail so much personal effort or risk for those who might be officially engaged in other activities.

Regional Exploration and Brokerage

The development of regional organization has been retarded in part by fear among existing political entities that new regional governments would usurp their powers of decision making and implementation. For this reason, although regional centers and regional governments may eventually take on certain of these powers, a more successful approach to developing regional focus initially is to stress the functions of exploration and, with increasing experience, brokerage — functions that are severely lacking at these levels. These two functions are also highly enriching educational processes for technologists, planners, manufacturers, consumer groups, and constituents.

Regional exploration-brokerage centers could facilitate interaction among individuals, independent groups, private and public institutions, specialists, and planners in exploring issues in a broad, future-oriented manner that would enable the centers to identify and initiate needed studies and experiments but remain separate from decision making and implementation. Also, by assisting the flow of people, ideas, and information, both among different problem areas and among the different sectors of society, center members could actively disseminate their knowledge to the people of the region and, in particular, to planners. An important corollary to this exploration and dissemination role is the potential for regional centers to provide continuing education for specialists desiring to broaden their own expertise.

Meeting with others of similar interests but different backgrounds to examine problems — not as a crash program but as part of an organized ongoing program — is essential to developing the kind of problem-solving specialists our third century will demand. But it is just as essential to go where the problems are to uncover needs that don't show up in national statistics, editorials, or the reports of national centers. Often the particular local manifestation of a problem has in it the nucleus of a successful solution. Fifty to a hundred such local solutions could, like a floodlight, illuminate new principles for solving similar problems in other places or at other levels.

Experimentation on an increased and broader scale seems essential in solving our social problems, but experimentation implies the need for accommodating failure as well as success. In fact, as in our technical laboratories, the absence of failures might well suggest that we are not being experimental enough. But failure, of course, must be at a level that avoids catastrophic or serious harm. This requires not only good initial design, but the flexibility to halt or redirect some experiments in a timely manner. This kind of flexible response requires continual interaction and feedback among many levels of society. A network of regional centers would facilitate and accelerate the flow of feedback as well as contribute substantive input of its own.

A brokerage role, based on extensive personal contact and active coordinating and matchmaking functions (as in the highly successful agricultural extension services of the United States), is a crucial factor in information dissemination. A local ombudsman in such a role can go directly to the planning commission, proper local agency, or even the mayor. On the other hand, at a national level, no matter what your credentials, how stylish your clothes, or even if you pay your own way to Washington, the real problem is uncovering the appropriate individuals and agencies to contact. Even more difficult is the task of obtaining the necessary cooperation from the numerous groups involved in a particular problem. This strategic "finding" process requires talented and knowledgeable brokers who can serve as frontrunners for the regions they serve and catalysts for the problem-solving groups they put together.

Effective regional brokers could also promote constituency-building as a way to involve a wide spread of citizen groups as well as public and private institutions on different issues. An active broker can help initiator groups by maintaining up-to-date directories of individuals, groups, and institutions willing to pool their resources on specific problems or who desire to build their own constituencies. A network of regional centers that served this directory function could facilitate the finding and interconnecting of relevant groups and agencies nationwide.

To achieve broad cooperation on complex social issues in which the financial and personal risks may be large, the brokerage process may require means of operation beyond the art of persuasion. In many cases, the broker and the initiator group would be far more effective if the brokerage had funds of its own to inject into the process, thereby demonstrating commitment and a willingness to share the risks. Professor William Linvill (1970) suggests the term "catalytic brokerage" for the situation in which brokers invest their own relatively small funds to attract the more ample resources of governments and institutions.

Ultimately, regional centers must be based not only on a broad knowledge of technology but on knowledge of political, economic, sociological, and psychological realities as well. Thus, the new kind of brokerage they represent must pull together the traditional "two cultures" (the humanities and the sciences) and the two modes of thought they represent into a higher-level, more integrated academic and social curriculum. The synthesis, in effect, requires an entirely new kind of brokerage career.

Regional Outreach

Even if these kinds of centers should operate apart from decision making they can still become vital participants in their communities. We have mentioned their role in educating and reeducating specialists. We can also envision a role in the educational community at large: as a provider of resource people for classrooms at every level (elementary, secondary, community college, and university); as developers of educational materials on social issues; and as practical learning centers for student interns. Regional centers could also form links among planners, business people, independent action groups, and public officials, who could be brought together periodically for exchange and mutual learning.

Indeed, as a crucial part of such an outreach program, we can consider the current need for our elected representatives to have certain minimum training requirements beyond age and residency. To deal effectively with the difficult issues that face them in our socially conscious, high-technology age, our local, state, and national representatives need far more than our trust to operate effectively; they also need a high degree of know-how and information and, as a very minimum, some technical understanding of the fundamental issues. Although it may be impractical to impose specific experiential or training requirements on elected officials, many of whom have already achieved prominence in other activities, we could at least provide a suitable educational opportunity for them, to serve almost as a "new career" reentry program. A network of regional centers focused on the issues of the social curriculum would provide part of a "school for representatives" through which to expand their general knowledge or periodically to study intensively in their fields of legislative specialization.

Regional centers could also serve the important functions of illuminating new problems as they arise and bringing legislators closer to their constituents in a context of shared concern. And, by being open to legislative staff and officials of the executive branch, such centers would serve as another source of input to legislative committees and administrative appointees.

SEARCH FOR A MODEL

The evolution of well-functioning centers is a long-term process, but our need is equally long term. Private foundations, as well as such government agencies as the National Science Foundation, are now being forced to work out the "interface" between science and the people. Toward this end, it is important that these institutions develop the means for supporting the evolution and operation of the social curriculum just as, during the past half century, they found the means for legitimately supporting the development and continued operation of the academic curriculum. In short, these institutions could serve important entrepreneurial roles in developing the new institutions of the social curriculum. For example, they could support studies that examine the best ways to initiate different forms of regional centers and then facilitate experiments, either by creating entirely new institutions or by slowly shifting the focus of existing ones.

A number of foundation-supported centers, such as the Behavioral Sciences Center for Advanced Study in California, currently provide a valuable service to the academic community. By offering an idyllic setting for individual research, study, and writing away from daily pressures and in a context of broad expertise, these centers facilitate the flow of ideas within the academic community and encourage interchange and exploration among the disciplines.

The regional exploration-brokerage centers that we seek could be modeled initially on existing academic centers, although with several major differences: Members of the new centers would be chosen solely on the basis of regional needs, would participate for variable periods of time, and would be expected to make a strong outreach effort within the region rather than studying apart from the community at large.

Existing centers offer support for proven performers from any of the familiar academic disciplines. Our new centers, however, would derive their focus from the social curriculum and would offer support primarily from individuals who are working with systems of knowledge rather than in single subjects: land or water management, energy, waste disposal, mass transportation, communication systems, and so on. Further, academic prestige per se would not be a prerequisite for appointments to the center; rather, centers would seek out participants with the potential for regionwide problem solving in specific areas.

The period of appointment would not be based on the academic year but might be a week, a month, or several years, depending on problem needs. Shorter terms would allow continual renewal of the staff and the opportunity for inviting or exchanging persons with experience in other technical fields or from other regions. Eventually, it is likely that appointments to well-functioning regional centers would be sought after as sabbaticals of a new sort.

Whereas centers serving the academic curriculum are internally focused, centers serving the social curriculum would be externally focused, and members would spend much of their time in the region, developing outreach programs to familiarize themselves with regional needs as well as to share their expertise with the public. It would also be valuable for exploratory fellows to move among centers in the course of their appointment so as to facilitate the matching of portfolios of skills and institutions to a given need. A tightly coupled network among centers would provide the required conditions for such movement, as well as developing and maintaining common outreach linkages.

Because of the importance of its outreach function, a regional center could not be managed as a retreat or a hotel. Directors would require the ability and perseverance to actively recruit specialist fellows, to promote vital outreach operations, and to resist capture by advocacy and special interest groups while ensuring their contributions. Directors would also be aware of the needs and opportunities in other regions and, through the flow of individuals, facilitate a viable national linkage among regional centers.

Such centers would require a financial base large enough to accommodate the wide spectrum of functions described earlier. Specialists who deal directly with social issues can be considered, as we said, the "professors" of the social curriculum and may be supported accordingly. "Students" learning new system functions might pay their own way just as students in higher education currently support themselves. However, there is a similar logic in providing grants to assist with or cover expenses, especially for older learners who are changing careers or broadening their experiential base. Educationally oriented regional centers, as a part of the new social curriculum system, could logically receive grants from foundations and government agencies, and companies could support employees at such institutions just as they support employees now at purely academic institutions. Students involved in center teaching activities could also earn stipends as at a university.

A university's accountability is measured by its accreditation standing, but accountability for institutions involved more closely with social issues would undoubtedly have other components. For example, a board of directors broadly representing the public, private, and independent sectors is a likely requirement, with numerous possibilities for wide representation.

In short, our society needs, and can afford to evolve, institutions that serve the broader social curriculum — like centers of the sort described here — just as it helped to evolve, and through a wide range of mechanisms currently supports, institutions that serve the underlying academic curriculum.

The vastness of our society, if nothing else, demands that we achieve a workable balance between centralization and decentralization in tackling our problems. The best centralized government can only in part compensate for weak local and state government, just as good local and state government can only in part compensate for weak central government. A network of learning centers and supporting facilities—similar to the regional exploration-brokerage centers discussed here—by serving as an interfacing layer between national centers and the public, could contribute to this critical third-century need.

IV

DISTRIBUTING SOCIAL GOODS: TRAVELING SHOWS

*America is groping for a new sense of coming together, but bridging the gap between isolated expertise and the public will require much greater awareness on both sides. To try to achieve increased awareness solely through **nonparticipatory** means such as TV documentaries, books, and lectures is not likely to be effective in itself. Traveling Chautauqua shows helped bring the America of 1900 together in thought and laughter. Now, in the 1980s, when the population is three times as large and the problems are, if not more intense, more complex and baffling, the face-to-face interaction and sharing that form the essence of traveling shows would be even more beneficial.*

Mixing entertainment with information and two-way communication, such shows would both dispense and collect information as they toured the country. Interaction could take place by means of exhibits and booths, video theaters, computer simulation systems, mobile bookstores and libraries, talks and debates, drama, and other forms of presentation. The national network formed by such traveling shows would be, in effect, a distribution system supporting and drawing support from the fixed local, regional, and national centers described previously.

Local and regional centers could provide us with much needed access to knowledge and media resources and could be an important step toward filling in the "empty middle" of our social marketplace. Nonetheless, we also need those complementary mechanisms that make it possible for us to interact with and "talk back" to our sources of information in order to achieve an active understanding of complex issues.

A marketplace that helps us cope with issues and that provides better access to the information we need requires far more direct channels of communication than are offered by newspapers, radio, or television. The media can give us the ideas of experts, but they are one-directional communications—we can't talk back or experience fields of expertise first hand. We need a way to choose what and when we want to learn and a means of participating in dialog with resource people in ways that answer our concerns and increase our understanding.

Often issues go across our television screens so quickly and in such highly polished form that we cannot grasp their content, let alone consider their potential implications or solutions. We need to be able to stop now and then and focus on a problem, learn about it, talk back to the experts, and try to understand the courses of action open to us. We also need to get out of our living rooms and libraries and directly experience social issues, together with people with similar concerns.

Unfortunately, individuals rarely have an opportunity to track the development of new systems such as nuclear power, solar energy, cable-TV, mass transportation, solid waste disposal, or computer-aided education, except perhaps as ultimate consumers. Yet we are asked to consider and to vote—directly or indirectly—on the future of many of these systems. However, without any first hand contact these systems remain highly abstract. Few of us need to master the details of such technical systems, but greater direct experience would demystify them and help bring them within our grasp.

Conventions and conferences are existing ways of meeting some of these needs—but only for select audiences and only in a one-shot, one-location format. As an alternative, we have some historical models for traveling shows that reached much larger audiences and provided entertaining forms of issue education.

TRAVELING CHAUTAUQUAS

A thousand years ago, Chinese caravans brought silks and porcelains to Europe, but they delivered more than these goods by the time their trip was completed. They picked up spices in India, sugar in the Levant, and new and different ideas all along the way, which they also spread through Europe. Similarly, 75 years ago, Chautauqua shows crisscrossed the United States, bringing culture, knowledge, entertainment, comedy, and excitement to small towns linked only by dirt roads or train tracks. The Chautauquas were an organized outgrowth of the large number of entertainers, lecturing humorists, dramatists, and moralists who individually toured the country as one-person shows during the nineteenth century. By merging comedy and culture and by organizing the routes over which they traveled, Chautauquas were able to attract large enough audiences to pay for impressive traveling companies. At the height of their popularity, hundreds of traveling companies served close to 10,000 communities, and many of the show groups contained from 100 to 200 people.

The following excerpts from the introduction to Harry P. Harrison's *Culture under Canvas* suggest the flavor of these traveling shows:

> Chautauqua tents rolled back and forth and up and down America for nearly thirty years. Pitched in pastures, school yards and courthouse squares, they offered not only the soaring oratory of a William Jennings Bryan, but also music, drama, magic, art lessons, cooking classes, low comedy and high-minded debates. Millions of eager listeners under the "big top" canvas, hot with summer's sun, perspired freely and soaked up both erudition and amusement.

> Famous men and women, statesmen and politicians, explorers and adventurers, actors and opera stars, heroes and an occasional well-publicized heel, each season covered the long summer trail. . . . "The most American thing in America," Theodore Roosevelt called it, a statement that few tried to challenge in the first quarter of the century.

> Those persons old enough to remember it think fondly of the frosting on this Chautauqua cake and forget the intellectual calories underneath. They remember the handsome Singing Hussars, the *Mikado* opera companies, the magician's white rabbits or the cute little number with blond curls singing *Tipperary,* and forget the debates, the arguments over legislation.

> Men talked freely from this new, informal platform. . . . Sponsors of daring ideas uttered them freely and all America went home to think. . . . The America that watched the first Chautauqua tent rise in an Iowa meadow in 1904 and the America that saw the last tent come down, twenty-nine years later in a little Illinois village, were separated by a period that marked swift changes in a people's thinking, in concepts of both humor and morality, in public and private manners. (1958, pp. xvi-xviii)

Joseph Gould, reflecting on the movement from the perspective of the 1960s in his *The Chautauqua Movement,* notes:

> It was praised for having done more toward keeping American public opinion informed, alert, and unbiased than any other movement, and in retrospect the judgement seems fair. Traveling Chautauqua brought to the attention of millions of Americans an impressive number of new ideas and concepts, many of which might never have received the popular support that guaranteed their acceptance. The graduated income tax, slum clearance, juvenile courts, pure food laws, the school lunch program, free textbooks, a balanced diet, physical fitness, the Camp Fire Girls, and the Boy Scout movement — all these and many more were concepts introduced by circuit Chautauqua. (1961, pp. 81-82)

MODERN TRAVELING SHOWS

Individuals in modern America are again very isolated, as in the era of the Chautauquas. The isolation stems from the inability to communicate with or to influence in a significant way centers of advanced knowledge, power, and policy making. Modern traveling shows, borrowing on the Chautauqua idea, could serve a critical distribution function between specialized knowledge on the one hand and local planners, leaders, institutions, and individuals on the other. By facilitating face-to-face interaction between different kinds of specialists and the communities, traveling shows could be a vital bidirectional link. They could bring information to the people and to all levels of decision makers, and could bring important feedback into the specialists' processes — something remote, one-way, and highly programmed TV cannot begin to achieve, and which public higher education is not designed to achieve.

The traveling shows we envision would be built on a broad base of interactive exhibits and booths (as in a typical professional convention), video theaters, computer simulation systems, mobile bookstores, talks and debates, and other such elements. They would not quite be trade fairs, county fairs, or professional conventions, but would incorporate important elements of each:

- A trade fair is focused on equipment and sales; our show would be focused on issues and ideas.
- A county fair is organized to entertain; our traveling show would inform in an entertaining way.
- A typical convention is structured for specific professionals; our show would be designed to communicate with nonprofessionals as well as professionals from many fields.

With a large-scale traveling show, communities could pool their experiences and avoid expensive mistakes. (Consider, for example, the recent problems of several communities that ended up being served by different cable-TV franchisers with incompatible equipment because of insufficient study and scattered decision-making processes.) The large size of traveling shows made possible by pooled resources could also assure the widest participation of all sectors of society. In a show on cable-TV, for example, the private sector could set up technical demonstrations; public agencies could demonstrate how other programs, such as satellite transmission systems, new educational technologies, and automated libraries, might interface with cable-TV systems; and independent groups could express constituents' concerns. In turn, specialists from different disciplines and geographic areas traveling together could gain insight and experience into community perceptions of given problems and their processes for meeting these problems, meanwhile learning from each other about vital aspects of issues that are new to them.

ASPECTS OF A TRAVELING SHOW

A traveling show could be to society what a convention is to an organization of specialists—an important means of *face-to-face* communication. When a specialty is changing quickly, conventions are likely to be frequent because change in any complicated activity contains many elusive elements that cannot be sensed solely from journal articles or other impersonal communications. Any convention-goer understands that a large part of convention business is conducted in small, informal working groups, over cocktails or dinner, where each person can better "sniff out" new concepts, connections, and configurations of ideas and people.

These convention elements are also important for the community education process we seek, but with some major differences. First, the usual business, professional, or academic convention deliberately detaches itself from the everyday life of the city that accommodates it. In an effective traveling show, however, the community itself would have to become an organic part of the proceedings if interaction between specialists and local officials and citizens is to take place.

Second, a modern traveling show would be a give-and-take, teach-and-learn enterprise. A part of its purpose would be to learn as it moved, gaining insight into what problems were common and general (though perhaps perceived as unique by a community), and what special situations existed.

Third, a show that travels throughout a region could engage the attention of the local and regional media and of the public more easily than a specialized convention or meeting. Wider media coverage and involvement would sharpen the recognition of the traveling show as a distinguished, "mustn't miss" enterprise, rather than just another show in town.

With a shift from a professional/client relationship toward more of a marketplace context for social planning and with much greater demand for open decision making on public matters, companies as well as government agencies face a new kind of selling situation. Such programs as water projects, antipollution systems, nuclear power plants, or mass transportation systems must be sold not only to the direct purchasers of such systems on the basis of their effectiveness or economy, but to the people as well.

A show focused on a topical issue — for example, mass transportation — could attract the participation of companies and government agencies with a message to convey, just as companies currently seek out and participate in trade fairs. Such participation would be important in developing a show of adequate scope and in covering the great costs involved in bringing comprehensive and highly focused educational shows to the public.

The ability to mix the entertaining with the intellectually stimulating would be critical. If the show were purely intellectual, the general public would not be attracted. If it were purely entertaining and commercial, specialists and policy makers would not become involved.

The potential audience can be thought of in several categories. Some will come because of professional or personal interest in the particular issue. Some will come because they would like to become professionally or personally involved in the future — perhaps in one of the satellite services spawned by any new technology. Some will come simply because the show sounds interesting. Still others will attend because their children have become intrigued as a result of a class visit. Indeed, organized tours from elementary and secondary schools would be likely to guarantee a large attendance base in each area the show visited.

People flock to auto shows, boat shows, and housing fairs. (Over 15 million people are on fairgrounds in California alone each year.) If the public developed a habit of attendance at these new shows, we could over time distill the major issues, tradeoffs, comparative costs, and side effects of any particular issue so as to cope with the choices ahead and develop the art of making valid inputs. In any case, Americans in our third century would have the exposure which, like the old Chautauquas, creates an "informed, alert, and unbiased" public opinion.

DEVELOPING A MODEL

Once traveling shows have caught on, any subject might be appropriate. Initially, however, the show probably would be best suited to topics for which there is general agreement in principle but no clear basis of comparison among methods (solid waste disposal, for example) and those in which the basic issues are just becoming apparent (such as mass transportation or energy). Topics, such as energy alternatives, that lend themselves to a broad range of physical displays are easiest to structure for high entertainment value.[1]

Location and Physical Setup

A traveling show would provide the public with a synthesis, in one place, of many kinds of events and exhibits (hardware) related to a particular issue. It would also provide an excellent context for meetings of local interest groups, city and regional specialists and local planners, or a representative and his constituents. In this context, participants could explore simultaneously the physical, technical, and social aspects of a particular issue.

To emphasize local focus, a traveling show might wisely use a combination of a centrally located community center, exhibit hall, library, school auditorium, or portable geodesic dome (perhaps the modern counterpart of the Chautauqua tent). County fairgrounds and community convention and exhibit halls would be even more useful since they have permanent staffs and are used to handling crowds and the accompanying traffic. They can also handle any variety of equipment and materials, including the trailer-based vans that many companies and

---

[1]To explore in this direction, the author has become connected with Energy Fair Foundation, whose predecessor organization, Energy Fair, Incorporated, since 1976, has presented an annual Energy Show involving exhibits from hundreds of large and small companies, independent groups, and state and federal agencies. It is an educational and entertaining show broadly focused on alternative energy sources and energy conservation. In the future, ways will be explored for moving small portions of such a show continuously throughout the year, in the spirit of the earlier traveling Chautauqua shows.

agencies are currently using for educational purposes but that crisscross the country independently without a suitable performance area or place to park. Issue-focused shows would seem an ideal context in which to group these mobile displays and exhibits.

County fairgrounds are also particularly appropriate because they are perceived as part of the community and offer great flexibility in organization. A show on energy, for instance, could be organized by focusing each building on a different energy source—solar, water, electric, nuclear, geothermal, wind, oil, and coal. Alternatively, the focus in each building could be on alternative energy uses—private and industrial transportation, private and industrial heating, energy uses in industry—or on the transfer of energy from the point of production to the point of use.

Show Components

Technical Sessions. In addition to comprehensive exhibits and displays and the usual "booths" of conventions and trade fairs, any complex issue would also warrant a number of special sessions on topics within that issue. A show on the topic of cable television, mentioned earlier, might have sessions on the legal and practical aspects of franchising; such social issues as free community channels, fee mechanisms, and ownership patterns; potential user groups; and hardware development and alternative technical schemes.

Films and Video Theater. An enormous amount of audiovisual material is available on almost every major issue, and a continuous showing of scheduled films throughout a show would be of great use to professionals, teachers, students, and private citizen groups. Some large cities already have specialty video theaters that cater to the swelling number of amateurs and professionals who deal in this new medium. Video films in these theaters range from new video art forms to presentation of local issues and phenomena. This use of video theaters could beneficially be used in traveling shows also, adding vitality to the show as well as serving important educational functions.

Traveling Bookstores and Libraries. Just as book publishers typically use professional meetings for promotional activities, our form of show would provide an equally useful opportunity for traveling library/information stores.

In addition, a traveling show (in conjunction with regional and local centers) could continually catalog printed, audio, and audiovisual material that is relevant to the show's theme. The catalog would be an important source for local planners, citizen groups, and schools. Local bookstores, libraries, or museums that wanted to stock show-related materials or coordinate exhibits could also use the catalog as a major resource.

Computer Terminals. Computer terminals and simulation programs go a long way in combining the education and entertainment aspects of a given issue. Exotic simulation games already exist in a number of different computer-based systems and could be used to illustrate the effects of population growth on transportation, energy, or waste disposal, for example, or perhaps the consequences of a certain level of energy growth.

Scheduling

Chautauqua circuits usually spanned the two to three months of the summer, and individual shows typically lasted a full week. Today, particularly because of the strong link that can be made with schools when they are in session, nonsummmer scheduling would seem more appropriate, at least initially. Summer time, on the other hand, is a convenient period for grant-supported work by teachers and students in creating exhibits, educational material, and audiovisual or computer simulation programs for the subsequent year's program. A range of student internships, in fact, is another potential employment/career opportunity of such shows.

Organized tours from elementary and secondary schools would logically account for a large part of daytime attendance at a show. (Emphasizing local school involvement could be doubly valuable: Besides the high educational value, enthusiastic students are likely to encourage parents to attend and help build show audiences.) Scheduling meetings and special sessions for late afternoon and evening would maximize the possibility of community attendance and would provide good timing for live broadcasting of selected events. In this manner, show participants, particularly those from distant places, might also have a chance to do regular-hours business in and around the community and region.

GETTING STARTED: THE IMPRESARIO

Some day there may well be a network of troupes, each focused on a different issue, traveling simultaneously in many parts of the country and served by many kinds of impresario institutions. But how do we start?

An initial investment is an obvious requirement. A consortium might provide the investment, perhaps as a joint venture of a state or federal agency, a foundation, and an independent organization. But beyond the financing is the need for a group or institution in an impresario role to help transform the idea of a traveling show into a reality. Much like the brokers in regional centers, impresarios would fulfill a critical management function in bringing together professionals, communities, special interest groups, and financial support without becoming captive to any particular sector.

Among existing organizations, potential contenders for the impresario role include private companies, foundations, citizen groups such as the National League of Women Voters or Common Cause, universities and their extension services, community colleges, planning agencies, professional groups, government agencies, research institutes, and individual citizens. However, private companies in the impresario role would appear to be promoting products rather than ideas, professional organizations to be protecting jobs, and activist groups to be promoting their own special interests; foundations are not generally equipped to organize large-scale implementations; government agencies would not be trusted in the present political climate; and universities would be vulnerable to criticism for diluting their teaching efforts, although many universities are equipped to organize and sustain large-scale operations through their extension divisions, which have experience and expertise in organizing programs throughout their state. Among existing organizations, nonprofit research institutes, which are organized for public service, and university extension divisions—both of which have a potential connection with essentially every governmental agency, every major industry, and every professional organization, but belong to no one—seem likely contenders for a primary management role.

Research institutes and university extension units that took on a primary impresario role, perhaps together, would profit by a greater awareness of community planning and decision-making processes, and staff members would also benefit through closer contact with public agencies, private companies, different stakeholder groups, the general public, and participating specialists from all parts of the country (and the world).

Any institution acting as impresario can appear to be advocating some particular position and be subject, therefore, to accusations of bias. However, if impresario institutions are successful in bringing together the broadest representation of all sectors, the greatest objectivity will be possible. Furthermore, when there are five, ten, or even fifty troupes touring the country with one particular topic, chance imbalances and weaknesses will cancel each other out across shows and through interaction with communities.

A network of impresario institutions would form a social circulatory system for facilitating the flow of people and ideas and would be able to coordinate the interactive aspects of different show issues. Eventually, a successful revival of the traveling show mechanism would require the development of a new and extensive system of travel and booking agents and the associated industry. This would represent yet another opportunity for private and commercial enterprise.

There seems little question that the social marketplace will require a distribution system of this type. Hundreds of shows traveling simultaneously—as in the days of the Chautauquas—each focused on a different issue or set of issues, would provide the social marketplace with an effective distribution system for pulling together disparate elements of the society in continuing dialog and problem-solving debate.

V

MULTISECTOR ORGANIZATION:
CONSORTIA

As the physical goods marketplace in America evolved, broad-based cooperation among individuals became crucial for production efficiency. Over time, corporate entities evolved that could accommodate this higher level of cooperation, both in shared stock ownership and shared work experience. During that period, industrial development was—as it still is—driven by hopes of maximizing production and the development of new products. Producing whatever is possible and profitable has been the underlying ethic of an intense period of industrialization. The next hundred years will necessarily be guided by greater focus on how to adapt technology and products to the functional needs of people, rather than making people adapt to a continuous unplanned stream of products.

It is futile as well as wasteful for product-oriented companies to address such broad societal needs as health care, transportation, communication, housing, or pollution control in an individual, purely competitive mode. Like America's space program, many of these programs demand broad cooperative effort and management. In our third century, as our focus shifts more to social functions, we will need a still higher level of grouping that can provide a structure for new kinds and levels of cooperative effort among companies, institutions, individuals, and independent groups. Forms of exploratory, limited-term, multisector consortia that address major societal functions would be an important and positive step in that direction.

The goal of placing a man on the moon was easily understood by the participants because it presented a specific technical problem. When we talk of adjusting highly interactive societal systems, however, our goals cannot even be stated in simple terms nor can our problem-solving approach be simplified to a clear step-by-step process. In tackling our social problems, we will need broad-based exploration and cooperation of the highest degree.

Consider, for instance, our present problems of inefficient energy use and vehicle-induced air pollution. We have yet to solve this dual issue satisfactorily. Giving up personal automobiles is not presently acceptable: We wouldn't like to take a sick child to the doctor on a bicycle, nor would we expect salespeople with heavy sample cases to make their rounds by bus, or rural families to make 30-mile shopping trips by taxi. Government regulation alone can't solve the problem, nor do we expect private industry to take the lead in making changes, since its profits are maximized by using existing standardized equipment, designs, and techniques.

We might, however, cut across conventional sector borders and bring together a consortium of transportation equipment companies, city and town governments, state and federal transportation specialists, and independent organizations, who could advance funds and resources to explore together transportation systems that would reduce air pollution, reduce energy and resource consumption, minimize solid waste, and improve transportation. Of course, the mere act of establishing a consortium — or even a network of consortia — would not automatically guarantee success, but this sort of breadth is critical if we hope to evolve satisfactory joint solutions to such complex issues in a timely manner.

DEVELOPING A MODEL

The essence of a post-industrial ethic is to adapt technology and products to the functional needs of people rather than making people adapt to the demands and consequences of a continuous unplanned stream of products.

The stock market offers a useful model for conceiving the shift from a focus on products to a focus on human functional needs. The stock market can be thought of as a highly distributed interconnection network serving many investors and many companies, as suggested on the left half of Figure 7. At any instant, each company has a constituency of stockholders, and each individual may own stock in many companies. By facilitating the exchange of stocks as well as the sale of primary stock, the market facilitates both the formation and readjustment of constituencies according to the continually changing needs and perceptions of both investors and companies.

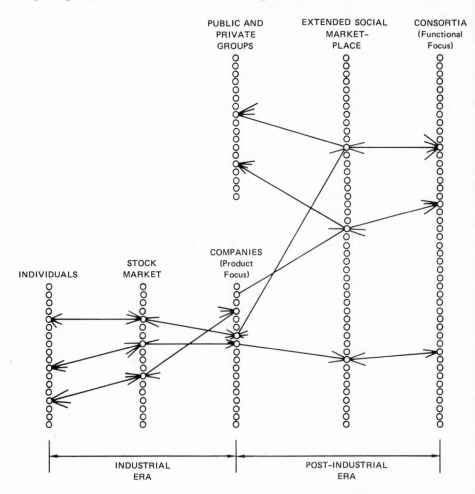

Figure 7   Extending organizational focus from product to function.

To serve its varied functions and preserve the fluidity of its constituent base, the stock market evolved a large range of services: brokerage and underwriting houses, legal and accounting services, mutual fund companies, report distribution services, company information resources, and investment counseling and other analytic services provided by the brokerage houses themselves. Through regional and local offices, it has developed outreach and presence; these facilities can serve tiny companies, industrial giants, very small investors, and large institutional investors with great flexibility and efficiency.

The extended social marketplace calls for carrying the constituency-forming process to a still higher level, as suggested on the right in Figure 7. To manage and guide the evolution of intricately interactive societal systems in a context of limited resources, we need extensive cooperation on problems that no single group, company, or institution has the skills, perceptions, and funds to tackle alone. Higher-level constituencies would have the potential for addressing social issues from a broad operational base and would provide each participating entity with increased perspective regarding current social needs and opportunities.

To serve its many functions, the extended social marketplace will require integration, outreach, credibility, and visibility comparable with those of today's stock market, while operating with great efficiency and incorporating a comparable range of services and skills. Like the stock market, the social marketplace must evolve a dense network of regional and local offices or centers, perhaps like those discussed earlier. Where the stock market has stockbrokers, the new market must develop social brokers. Where the major concern of the stock market is the economic profit and loss statement, the new market must be concerned with broader social accountability, possibly through such instruments as the "social profit and loss" statement. Where the stock market caters to financial entrepreneurs, the new market will cater as well to social entrepreneurs. Both markets trade in knowledge and information and, to be effective, both must invite and attract involvement.

Perhaps the most important aspect of the shift from competition among the small, independent, family-owned businesses of an earlier day to the present competition among corporations is that in the long run it took cooperation among many smaller units, initially individuals, to generate the corporate entities. In short, the shift to more efficient production came about through cooperation.

A still higher level of grouping, in turn, requires the cooperative efforts of companies, institutions, and independent groups. When we achieve this grouping, we will have not only a higher-level perspective, but also expanded activity among many consortia. In time, competing consortia would probably form within major social function categories (like health, transportation, energy, resources, or waste) just as companies compete now within major product categories (like electronics, computers, aerospace, automobiles, or drugs). Eventually, a company might have shares or an interest in different consortia, just as individual shareholders hold stock in different companies. Such ability to join different higher-level consortia could produce general social benefits by increasing institutional flexibility in a rapidly changing environment.

Term Consortia

Those who feel that many of our current social problems derive from corporations with power rivaling that of the state would deny that we should even imagine grouping institutions at a still higher level. And yet, if the social marketplace is to help us cope, it seems inescapable that we must permit — even encourage — higher-level groupings of the type outlined above.

However, our goals would probably best be served by consortia that were established for limited duration, and for a limited, specific purpose, rather than for growth or permanence. Each would address a particular problem, or cluster of problems, and would disband after a specified term. If need dictated, a new consortium could be formed to carry on. In effect, a term consortium would constitute a new form of "limited liability" entity, limited in lifespan as well as resource commitment.

Term consortia would allow each member institution to find out which groups worked well together before possibly taking steps toward a more permanent merger. Whether arranged for profit or not for profit, each member group could benefit from the increased insight and institutional flexibility that would accrue from working together with other operational entities in a semiformal way. Corporate subunits such as divisions could also benefit from consortia-type participation in the new marketplace. With rapid social change and, often, equally rapid change in corporate goals, some divisions of a corporation may no longer find a proper atmosphere for continued operation. As with larger consortium members, such subgroups could, through mutual exploration, gain a better perspective of the opportunities available and subsequently choose to change their structure, move on to some other configuration, or dissolve. In effect, we are considering a notion of portable groups and portable divisions.

Exploratory Focus

Consortia aimed at specific operational tasks are hardly novel. However, the kinds of consortia we are considering here would extend and support the *exploratory* in contrast to the *operational* function in the problem-solving process illustrated in Figure 3.

The output from a multisector exploratory consortium may take the form of recommendations for new types of products, new forms of systems, new research directions, or new legislation. Such consortia would have high educational value for all participants that could feed into long-range solutions.

Joint exploration can illuminate ways in which one industry's problems can become another industry's resource, thus eliminating waste in resources, efficiency, or money. Although it might require legislation to permit and even encourage new operating procedures, broad-based exploration is a first step in actively illuminating new legislative possibilities and in building widespread support for change.

The parties to such ventures might all be formal industrial enterprises, although in general they would be more likely to include groups from the public and independent sectors, such as nonprofit institutions, research foundations, universities, specialized communes, or private consumer groups. In the new, post-industrial society, the opportunity to become involved in new ways may be to some as important a reward for participation as profit is to others.

Higher-level organization in the private sector, though complicated by problems of industrial secrecy, large financial risk, and legal restrictions such as antitrust, would be much simpler with limited-term consortia organized for exploratory purposes. Also, such consortia would require less venture capital, where any is necessary, since funding need only support the new exploratory function. Where appropriate, investors might obtain warrants from participating companies, in addition to shares in the consortium in case it should accumulate assets such as copyrights, patents, or real property.

External Research and Development Function

Possible strategies for establishing a broad-based exploratory grouping range from outright acquisition of a set of companies to forming term consortia as discussed above. The difficulty with outright acquisition is that it would exclude public and independent groups and would require taking on new operational responsibilities that are basically antithetical to an exploratory mode. A term consortium, on the other hand, would be comparatively free from internal pressures toward operational goals and potentially more open to a wider set of participants. It would achieve, in effect, a form of external research and development function, separate from any one company or investor.

Consortia Management

The evolution of broad-based, exploratory consortia will require experimentation aided by new forms of brokerage and venture capital. Eventually, consortia management companies are likely to evolve that could pass on accruing knowledge to other groups in the same way that today's management consulting companies aid in the start-up and operation of individual companies.

However, consortia aimed specifically at social exploration contrast strongly with more familiar coalitions aimed at specific operational or implementation programs and therefore would require correspondingly different management skills. In a coalition addressing a typical operational problem, high commonality of language, knowledge, responsibility, and expertise is necessary so that specific commitments can be made quickly and easily. In an exploratory consortium, however, less commonality and overlap among participants would provide, among other advantages, a less competitive and therefore more open approach to exploration, as well as a wider sampling of the larger society. To achieve this kind of scope, flexibility, and openness, consortia managers would need to develop a larger focus on social functioning than is required of today's corporate managers and management consulting companies.

CONNECTION WITH THE MARKETPLACE

Consortia of private, government, and independent organizations could provide an important element of cooperative effort on complex social problems. However, it would be easier for these kinds of consortia to form and function effectively when other parts of the marketplace evolve further. For instance, traveling shows, regional centers, and exploratory consortia could be highly supportive of each other's functions: centers in finding and granting funds to help in the formation of multisector exploratory consortia; consortia by developing well-analyzed, possible alternative actions on major issues, helping such centers to promote exploration of issues; and traveling shows by serving a distribution function. The rich environment of supportive regional and local centers would help develop new market initiators, brokers, and consortia managers, as well as new venture capital investors.

Research into multisector consortia would help to pinpoint the best strategies for their formation, and the sorts of legislation and changes in legislation that may be necessary to permit such entities to function properly. As much as anything, however, perceiving a need for them in the future increases the emphasis on beginning to develop other parts of the marketplace that would contribute to effective consortia functioning.

HUMAN NETWORKS

Underlying the rapid growth of America during the last hundred years were the railroad, telegraph, telephone, automobile, airplane, radio, and electric power. Each is a large network and industry that, in turn, underlies many other industries. New technologies such as computers, television, cable-TV, and satellite broadcasting will add to our networking skills. But a network has meaning only in terms of what flows through it. In information networks, electronic signals, books, films, packages, and so forth flow through. Many engineers are now busily generating new and ever more complex electronic networks on the ground and in the sky. The main goal here, however, when we talk about higher-level groupings, or consortia, or certain kinds of centers or traveling shows, is energizing the flow of people, along with their ideas and concepts: the human network component.

VI
EXTENDING THE MARKETPLACE
INTERNATIONALLY

*Once we asked whether a nation so divided can long endure. Now we ask whether a **world** so divided can long endure. How can we promote greater international coordination and cooperation?*

Viewing the future through the filter of an expanding national social marketplace, we see the need ultimately to develop similar mechanisms at an international level, but over a much longer time scale and with a much greater variety of institutional forms. This chapter considers some major trends driving us in the direction of a global community and notes briefly some of the institutional forms that might soon be emerging necessities for coping with these trends.

Beyond the internal problems we are experiencing as a nation, we face fundamental, difficult, and critical international problems as well. Sharing food and equalizing standards of living are two of the most pressing international issues we face. In the past, we have borrowed from the Robin Hood legend, seeing ourselves as good-hearted souls who fight repression and act as agents for redistributing wealth. The Marshall Plan and the Agency for International Development (AID) are two formal channels through which we have played this international role.

Now, however, with our new awareness of resource limitations and the general impracticality of a simple system of taking from the "haves" and giving to the "have-nots," some people urge that the United States immediately adopt a "lifeboat philosophy." Proponents of this philosophy argue that we cannot possibly feed the population projected for the near future and that it is folly to be generous with food that will soon be precious. In fact, they say, by stimulating population growth in countries already incapable of feeding themselves, gifts of food aggravate the situation; others argue that we help to feed the world or lose both our humanity and our security. It is unlikely that either philosophy alone can serve us well in our third century, for our problems and interrelationships are changing as radically and rapidly as our domestic social needs. We will need a sophisticated system of international decision making that takes into account both the needs of individual nations and the larger needs of an emerging world network.

But complex issues always have many facets, and antagonists and protagonists often are guided by different images. To whom should we entrust critical international decisions? Businessmen? Generals? Politicians? Technologists? We cannot trust the decisions that will shape our future to any single individual, group, or nation. Nor do we want a "perfectly planned" future; we have seen how that, too, can lead to unanticipated and undesirable effects because we don't have enough understanding or control of our own social systems.

However, there is never a shortage of entrepreneurs and initiators who are willing to make decisions daily—decisions that commit people and resources and that can have important consequences. Myriad isolated decisions set patterns that ultimately will represent our answers and our decisions on the complex issues we face. To evolve decisions that we will be satisfied to live with requires new kinds of contexts in which a broad range of individuals can function: contexts that can illuminate new kinds of opportunities. Critical are contexts that are broader that those offered by the executive suites of multinational corporations, military planning centers, smoke-filled caucus rooms, or the garrets of revolutionaries. Equally critical are contexts that can develop relevant information and that can take account of cultural differences, as are contexts that facilitate the brokerage of broad-based consortia and nourish the exploration of common problems over long periods of time. In brief, we need new forms of international exchange.

PLANETARY CONSCIOUSNESS

The oneness of mankind is a perennial belief, and yet our daily experience continually reminds us that we still have far to go. At the same time, a body of common experience continually evolves. We share more than the dawn and the sunset; we share the same experience of tools, from hypodermic needles to tractors, and the same experience of television and radio. We make accommodations even with our adversaries so that phone calls can go through, airplanes can land, penicillin can be manufactured. Orbiting spacecraft and TV signals are not halted by international boundaries, and 35mm film and batteries for transistor radios are ubiquitous regardless of country. Similarly, ideas can no longer be contained within national boundaries, even with the aid of a strong secret police and constant purges.

As modern technology and commerce shrink the globe, we are more conscious than ever of the multitude of small nations, of the differences among cultures, of bits of information like the fact that there are hundreds of languages on the island of New Guinea. At the same time, it is only in this century that we have begun to speak of "world war." That term implies that we have developed interconnections and interactions in the most real way imaginable. Almost any nation can now destroy us all, either directly or by instigating such a war. If we do not have the power of life over one another, we do have the power of death.

Thus, even as we become conscious of our differences, the world is beginning to function as one entity. We realize the global nature of pollution; we speak of the world's food supply; we see wars between remote nations not just as threats to our system of alliances and our balance of power but as threats to our lives.

Centuries from now our descendants will record how humanity was able to move from a lifestyle of tiny isolated bands to a planetary community, not of uniformity, but of interwoven and interacting diversity. If this does not occur, little may be left to observe. In spite of the importance of succeeding, we cannot force agreement. The only action open to us is to build the organization and the institutions that will facilitate agreement and cooperation.

INCREASING THE COMMON BASE OF EXPERIENCE

Enhancing broad-based international exchange requires that we find ways to increase the common base of experience. Anyone who has seen people from different cultures growing up in harmony and trust knows that an adequate base of common experience lessens the fears and conflicts that can arise from dissimilarity. The basic goal is that of transcending barriers or bridging gaps between dissimilar social systems on a worldwide scale.

If nations with areas of deep mistrust and hate are to live together in a family of nations, areas of common experience *must* be developed. We suffer when each country propagates its own fixed tradition, just as we delay the development of new patterns by imprinting old patterns too strongly in children. Common experience increases the likelihood that people will be able to interpret the actions of others more realistically and thus be able to anticipate situations. Also, common experience allows the memory of trauma at the hands of one representative of a culture to become just one of many memories, and not the only memory that is transmitted. To develop new common experience, it is important to explore realms that are not governed by rigid tradition; that is, it is best to aim toward border-transcending rather than border-breaking processes; new experiences should be based as much as possible on new ideas, projects, goods, and social values rather than the usual economic and political concepts on which the present borders depend.

Boundaries serve the function of facilitating a continual evolution of new social forms, in the sense that each society is a social experiment.

But deep, isolating boundaries can become more permeable and allow freer passage of individuals and ideas, as in the European Economic Community, without losing this function. The advantage of permeability is suggested by analogy with nonpermeable membranes, which rupture when the difference in pressure on the two sides of the membrane becomes too great. Permeable membranes, in contrast, allow pressures to equalize while staying intact.

Isolation allows a cultural skin to form, and within the privacy of that encasing skin, institutions tend to condition people to be of similar kind. In his book *The Mature Mind,* H. A. Overstreet discusses the immaturity and danger of nationalism in the following way:

> In the modern world . . . most of the earth's inhabitants have been conditioned to the concept of nationalism. A man may be a man "for a' that"; but first of all, he is an American, a Russian, a German. We might more properly say, in the light of Pavlov's experiment, that modern man was born human, but that by a complex reiterated "meat-and-bell" technique he has been made into an American, a Russian, a German. (1949, pp. 30-31)

In isolation each group evolves differently, in effect becoming a different social species. Just as a human is uneasy in the presence of a dangerous animal whose behavior he cannot predict, so one human group is uneasy in the presence of a potentially dangerous group whose behavior is not understood. Russians are different from Americans, Israelis are different from Arabs, and East Pakistanis are different from West Pakistanis. The difference lies primarily in their accumulated experience; that is, in their memories. What we must search for are ways to increase the level of common experience and to bridge the gaps between these culturally isolated social systems.

An extraterrestrial political scientist might view political Earth, with its strong isolating boundaries, much as an earthly physicist views a piece of magnetic material: as a system of domains, within each of which there is strong coherence. In the case of a magnetic material, the net magnetic direction varies from domain to domain, and it is the total pattern of domains that constitutes the overall "memory state." The ability to change the domain pattern easily, and hence the memory state, is what underlies the great utility of these magnetic components in computer memory systems. One can effectively change the memory state of such a material in two ways: by applying a certain amount of heat or by an external magnetic field.

Although neither process can be directly translated to such a highly evolved form as a society, the analogy can shed some light. To change the memory pattern of societies, one could deliberately try to "heat" the political world through terrorism. However, whereas a magnetic material can survive a succession of intermediate "undesirable" states, human society is much more fragile and is capable of self-destruction on the way to some envisioned "perfect" state.

Application of an external magnetic field is analogous to world conquest; the conqueror tries to enlarge his domain until the entire world is "polarized" or oriented in the same direction. This strategy is no longer acceptable because of the risks involved. With the current level and distribution of world armaments, the destruction that would accompany such attempts would dwarf the tragedy of two world wars.

If we do not wish to heat up the world further or align all domains in the same direction, we can instead lower the barriers and permeate the domain walls, developing controlled flow across boundaries, building more dimensions of exchange and, therefore, greater connectivity. We can allow memories and experiences to interact in a controlled flow: fast enough to cause change but not so fast as to generate undue heat.

International flow evolves from all manner of interaction and exchange programs, from world fairs and Olympic Games, from international science organizations, from attempts to form international agreements, from multinational corporations, from activities of the United Nations. Each of these makes its contribution, one way or another, but separately, in isolation. The current context does not nurture and support the connections that develop. Sporadic, short-term interactions among small groups of specialists are important but not sufficient. We need to plant the seeds of awareness much more extensively and in many different combinations—primarily by working on common problems.

The multidisciplinary approach is hailed in the United States as a way to generate broader-based expertise in technology and in social problem solving. A goal of incorporating elements of multiple cultures in the same persons, in order to achieve a new social synthesis, would be in the same spirit as technological fusion, where individuals specialize not simply in mathematics or physics but in mathematical physics, or physiological psychology, or quantum electronics, or bioengineering. These higher-level or transcending bridges do not destroy the generative fields, but rather enhance them.

THE DRIVING FORCE

To illuminate the nature of the institutions that we may require, let us consider the nature of some of the forces that are driving us toward greater international interaction.

A New Meaning for Political Borders

American political borders, though geographically well defined, are readily crossed. The border between New York and New Jersey demarcates two distinct political units, but cars, trains, television programs, and airplanes cross it with ease. The border between California and Oregon indicates a change in road sign conventions, paving type, and sales tax, but people flow easily between the two states. Borders between nations, on the other hand, represent more rigid demarcations. The border between West Germany and East Germany is fenced, mined, and patrolled, and is practically impermeable to most visitors, refugees, or currency; any attempt to penetrate this border by military means would lead to a rupture that would damage not only the two Germanys, but perhaps all of Europe and much of the rest of the world as well.

Technology is changing the meaning of national borders, however. The border between West Germany and East Germany *is* permeable to radio waves, TV programs, and weather and communication satellites; and no kind of border will stop smog, nuclear fallout, intercontinental ballistic missiles, or orbital weapon systems. The burning of high-sulfur coal in Great Britain and the Ruhr can produce an acid rain in Sweden. And new technology is continuing to weave an ever-tighter international fabric, requiring new kinds of international agreement that will eventually redefine what we mean by political borders.

Leo Szilard, in his book *The Voice of the Dolphins* (1961, p. 65), fantasizes a scenario in which Russia finally resolves the German-Polish problem by offering Poland 3- to 10-mile-wide strips of land on its eastern border each year for twenty five years on condition that Poland cede, year by year, similar strips of land on her western border to Germany, with due compensation to all people and to all countries involved — a tongue-in-cheek but fascinating proposal. We sense, however, that there would be greater stability if imaginary lines drawn on the map of the earth's surface were not so crucial to begin with.

Greater Visibility and Vulnerability

During its second century, America—along with Europe and, later, Japan—uncritically pursued technological progress. We regarded the social consequences as the inevitable price of progress and as a result created serious resource and environmental problems for ourselves. The new forms of wealth generated by technology also pulled technological countries farther away from the others, widening the gap between the world's haves and have-nots in per capita income, life expectancy, and use of resources.

Our technological progress has also yielded instruments of communication that make the world into a theater with all *good* seats. Telstar and worldwide TV have shown the have-not nations just what there is to want or not want, as well as exposing all nations to greater international scrutiny. We have developed new kinds of weaponry and made possible terrorist tactics that can hamstring the powerful and give the weak the power of extortion. Modern industrial states no longer have a monopoly on world influence and are increasingly being called on to attend to the demands of smaller nations or even of guerrilla bands.

In *The War of the Flea* (1970), Robert Taber suggests that this increased vulnerability of modern industrial states results in large part from their dependence on masses of workers and an intricate web of machinery and institutions, all of which must function if the system as a whole is to function:

> [T]hey must, at all costs, keep the economy functioning and showing a profit or providing the materials and markets on which another, dominant economy depends. Again, they are vulnerable because they must maintain the appearance of normalcy; they can be embarrassed out of office. And they are triply vulnerable because they cannot be as ruthless as the situation demands. They cannot openly crush the opposition that embarrasses and harasses them. (pp. 25-26)

This dependence on maintaining large bulky systems places considerable power in the hands of guerrillas, who have less to defend and therefore can risk more:

> The guerrilla fights the war of the flea, and his military enemy suffers the dog's disadvantages: too much to defend; too small, ubiquitous, and agile an enemy to come to grips with. (p. 29)

By an analysis of recent revolutionary wars throughout the world, Taber concludes that

[T]he war of the flea, as it is seen today, is not merely popular war, but the war of the world's *have-nots,* the natural weapon [i.e., guerrilla warfare] lending itself to the situation of subjugated and exploited peoples everywhere. In short, it is a revolutionary weapon. (p. 150)

Because great industrial states can no longer easily dominate the poorer ones, and because the elite of an industrial society can no longer so easily oppress the poor or disenfranchised within it, greater international cooperation is crucial for the survival of both haves and have-nots. The Vietnam War made these points clear to America, and comparable experiences have brought on similar new awareness in other industrial nations as well.

Multinational Corporations

Another force taking us in the direction of higher-level agreements and organization is that of the multinational corporations. These corporations transcend national boundaries, facilitating trade in highly skilled management services as well as in goods and capital. The global or multinational corporation represents a worldwide capitalism with new and profound consequences. As multinationals increase and as they invent more and more ways to balance risk and reward, they will pose problems that will demand new solutions.

Multinational corporations are beginning to repeat on an international level the enormous growth of the private sector that we experienced within the United States during our second century. Just as we were confronted then with a burgeoning private sector that could transcend state boundaries and plan on a national scale, we see now the emergence of a powerful international private sector that can transcend national boundaries and plan on an international scale. Growth of the U.S. government arose in large part to check and regulate the spread of centralized big business, which operated on a national level; in a still distant future, we can visualize a period when a highly centralized international government may also be necessary to counterbalance a highly centralized international private sector, which is now in its infant stages; and, to take our analogy one step farther, we may find that a potent international independent sector will finally emerge to rebalance the powerful international private and public sectors. Such a rebalancing might represent the final act in establishing a true international, planet-wide cooperative society. In the meantime, it is perhaps ironic, but true, that while we seek to decentralize nationally, we must simultaneously become more centralized (coordinated) internationally.

DEVELOPING MECHANISMS FOR
INTERNATIONAL EXCHANGE

At this point in our history, we are still seeing the evolution of the isolated parts of an international social marketplace, and we must rely on fragments of information to give us the overview we seek. As one indicator of how far we have come, Quincy Wright notes that expenditures for general international organizations have increased tenfold every 25 years since the establishment of the International Postal Service in 1870 (Wright, 1964). As an indication of how far we have yet to go in developing effective mechanisms, however, we can compare the current total annual budget of the United Nations—some $500 million—with the total world spending for defense and armaments, which is approaching $500 billion. It would be a tremendous achievement if we could spend even half of what the world spends on armaments, which are usable only when all else fails, on mutual problem solving to assure that all else does not fail.

Our problems in uniting the numerous factions in the United States are magnified many times when we turn our attention to the diverse cultural forms and patterns that exist in the world. Until well into this century, for example, it was against the law in parts of Afghanistan to teach that the world is round; and in Chad, the educated urbanized elite have been subjected to severe rituals to purge them of their Western ways. We cannot, therefore, expect the institutions we project for our internal social marketplace to evolve soon in many other parts of the world or to take on the same forms we develop. Nonetheless, as long as the political and cultural price is not too high, we can expect most people, regardless of cultural background, to want a supply of pure water (once they know it is possible) or to want houses that don't crush them in an earthquake; and we will need international mechanisms for transferring purification and construction methods, and similar transferable knowledge, from culture to culture. The diversity in national needs and access to knowledge resources require very different strategies and timing in different places, but the eventual establishment of many kinds of international centers worked out among nations could greatly enhance the international flow of information and technology, promote understanding of and respect for cultural differences, and minimize the impediments created by such differences.

In *Small Is Beautiful: Economics as If People Mattered* (1973), E. F. Schumacher, a British economist with long experience in developing countries, complains that economic aid to these countries typically strives for the instant creation of industry rather than for an evolutionary approach. However, no modern industry can develop or survive without an extensive base of infrastructure: educational institutions, transportation and communication networks, sources of banking and venture capital, research units, and some form of a modern physical goods marketplace.

Thus, to send a modern steel mill to a developing country as a *fait accompli* is to deliver only the tip of the iceberg and may well exacerbate existing problems if the groundwork has not been laid for the emergence of a modern sector. Untrained people who have little to do in a modern facility, for example, are enticed into the cities in massive migrations, bringing with them the potential for mass unemployment and subsequent alienation.

Schumacher argues instead for developing intermediate technologies that can create real jobs and help build infrastructure:

> The gift of knowledge [in place of goods] . . . has far more lasting effects and is far more closely relevant to the concept of "development." Give a man a fish, as the saying goes, and you are helping him a little bit for a very short while; teach him the art of fishing, and he can help himself all his life. On a higher level: supply him with fishing tackle; this will cost you a good deal of money, and the result remains doubtful; but even if fruitful, the man's continuing livelihood will still be dependent upon you for replacements. But teach him to make his own fishing tackle and you have helped him to become not only self-supporting, but also self-reliant and independent (1973, p. 186).

Skills Centers

A recent example of exporting "fishing tackle" without corresponding lessons in self-reliance is the National Academy of Sciences' attempt to spread the technology for ferrocement, a material composed of a dense meshwork of steel wire embedded in thin layers of cement (National Academy of Sciences, 1973). Ferrocement has great potential as an airtight and watertight material with wide applications in food and water storage and the construction of buildings and small boats and ships; the materials used are almost completely indigenous or readily available everywhere in the world, and the methods of application are labor-intensive, requiring relatively little capital investment. However, the means for transferring this technology to where it might be needed and to the ultimate user is lacking. It has become clear that merely publicizing the opportunity, writing reports, or holding technical conferences among professionals will not achieve the transfer.

Skill-transfer centers would be a stride in the direction of developing intermediate technology, in Schumacher's sense, and of building infrastructure. International centers for learning skills could provide an opportunity for individuals to learn the rudiments of a skill at a low cost, with periodic refresher courses to maintain and improve proficiency. Craftspeople could become "students" in centers for learning glazing, sewer pipe construction, electrical wiring, road construction, or the technology of ferrocement, and could return to their communities with heightened skills and new methods. By concentrating on the transference of skills rather than ideas or philosophy, such centers could exist with minimum threat to government units, and to that extent participants could return to their villages or communities relatively free of alienating ideologies or "culture shock."

Research Centers

In addition to the transfer of basic skills, we also need to develop mechanisms for international collaboration in uncovering common problems and potential solutions. The International Centre of Insect Physiology and Ecology (ICIPE), established in 1970 in Nairobi, Kenya, is one such multipurpose international research facility already in existence.

> [ICIPE] was designed to further development in East Africa; to foster the growth of the African scientific community by training research students at the postgraduate and postdoctoral levels; to encourage collaboration between senior scientists from developed countries and researchers from East Africa on projects of crucial importance to both groups; to contribute to the practical solution of pressing problems in local agriculture and health; to develop biological methods of insect control that are less dangerous than the highly toxic chemical pesticides; and finally . . . . to pursue advanced research in insect biology and related fields (American Academy of Arts and Sciences, 1972).

The center is supported by a number of international funding bodies, including the United Nations Development Program; the Dutch, Swiss and Japanese governments; AID; the Sloan and Rockefeller foundations; and the Commonwealth Fund.

We need similar centers throughout the world for joint research in such worldwide concerns as health, birth control, pollution prevention, agriculture, and energy systems. Centers would best be located near the point of need or in areas especially relevant to the research; ICIPE's location, for instance, makes it a year-round natural laboratory for the study of insects.

Regional Exploration Centers

Initial concentration on basic skills and specific research is appropriate in many parts of the world. In the more distant future, we can also visualize the establishment of exploration-brokerage centers serving different regions of the world.

As in America, regional centers could serve a dual purpose: as classrooms for the training of broad-based specialists and as brokers for a region. In some cases, a region might be geographically defined—for instance, the countries in the region surrounding the Mediterranean Sea, like the counties of the San Francisco Bay Area, should ultimately manage both the opportunities and problems offered by their proximity to the sea. In other cases, regional centers might be designed around problems common to developed nations, such as protecting water supplies from industrial pollution, or common to most nations, such as resource allocation.

In their brokerage role, regional centers might take responsibility for steering people to resources and to other people with common interests. International directories currently catalog statesmen, religious leaders, businesspeople, artists, athletes, and academicians. These directories could be augmented with inventories of people whose skills and experience lie in meeting more common needs, in addition to reflecting the more sophisticated and familiar areas of joint study and research.

Traveling Shows

Traveling shows may be an important distribution process for knowledge goods and services in the new marketplace, but it is difficult to conceive of initiating them worldwide until a larger body of common experience exists. Special situations, however, do exist, such as Project Hope, an international hospital and medical service ship, sailing from one nation's harbor to another. In any case, such shows cannot be imposed and expected to succeed; the need must first have been recognized.

It seems natural that such shows—which might be focused, for example, on new agricultural methods, pollution control, or energy alternatives — would evolve from successful international centers. Countries that saw such centers as both useful and unthreatening would be likely to provide the impetus to put specialized shows on the road in order to bring techniques, skills, and ideas to the point of application. In fact, international centers could serve as a theater route for traveling shows.

A Global Network

Although technology is under attack in many quarters, it has an important role to play in the new international marketplace. To become effective and to attract people from far away places, international centers will require an established store of media and knowledge resources and modern research facilities.

The Food and Agriculture Organization of the United Nations is a potential network of centers of the type envisioned. It is not really an aspect of world government, but it is an embryonic information and brokerage center with a specific focus. As we approach a crisis period in the world production and distribution of food, the importance of the FAO should increase as rapidly as the urgency of its mission.

Suppose the FAO established an electronic communications system with its remote regional offices. This system might provide output or information display terminals in the central office in Rome. Reports from various countries would be translated and entered into the system so that every individual at the regional center had access to the information developed. Questions about techniques could be answered in minutes instead of weeks. Even with crude computer models stored in the system, a regional FAO mission could get an idea of some of the likely results of a twenty percent decrease in the grain crop in its own region, or the effect on its region of a sudden drought in another region. Through cooperation with other agencies, such as the agency that provides weather satellite information, it would begin to be possible to institute a food and agriculture early warning system so that India could know, for example, that its own drought coincided with a bumper rice crop in the Philippines or a shortened growing season in the Canadian wheat belt.

A mission control center, like the one that guided our Apollo space flights, stirs an image of great efficiency and almost absolute confidence. Such a center seems like a crowning achievement of technology applied to a purely technological problem. Mission control centers applied to social needs, on the other hand, are likely to evolve very slowly because the very kinds of information needed can have great political impact and are therefore highly guarded. But nations are nevertheless working toward constructing a worldwide communication and information system; and, with time, more and more relevant information will naturally enter these networks. During the building period, some people will be hypnotized by the technology itself. However, when substantial portions of the network are in place, the technology will fade into the background, like the telephone system, and be appreciated for what it is—an underlying structure that facilitates the exchange of information and ideas and, therefore, mutual decision making.

The Cost Is Small

How do you measure cost-effectiveness? We often become trapped into very detailed readjustments of budgets but are stunned at the gross imbalances in the overall budget when we stand back for a broader view. The world can eventually afford a large number of centers that facilitate our working directly on common problems rather than continuously working around their edges. At present, we act as though giving a problem a name and mentioning it often enough will magically give us control over it, and we devote millions to exploring the edges. Even a thousand such centers at an average annual cost of $10 million each would represent only a couple of percent of the current world armaments budget!

PERSPECTIVE

A living organism is an entity composed of many parts mutually supportive of the whole. Proper functioning of the whole is necessary for the proper functioning of each of the parts. An amoeba is an organism, as is a human being; and, in its own way, a society is an organism. Each is composed of many mutually supportive parts, and the health of each part depends on the overall health of the organism.

When a human looks into a microscope, he can see some of the physical relationships of a biological organism, but what escapes him is the nature of life itself. He continually asks: What is the purpose of this act or that act? What guides the overall functioning of this organism? An extraterrestrial observer would feel the same bewilderment as he focused his "terrascope" on the large number of "cells" moving about on our planet Earth. What is the purpose of this act or that act? What guides the overall functioning?

Although we do not know the answers to such fundamental questions, we know nevertheless that organisms evolve. Cultures evolve too. In the beginning, man apparently lived in small, isolated hunting bands vastly different from modern societies numbering hundreds of millions of individuals. Although physical evolution is measured in millions of years and cultural evolution in tens, hundreds, and thousands of years, the changes that accompany cultural evolution are comparably complex. When we try to visualize how a particular biological organism evolved a certain new part or function, we find it difficult to trace in our mind just how so many already existing parts could have evolved in synchrony to this new level of organization. Many people are similarly concerned with how, or even whether, mankind now, with its many intensely competing and conflicting subcultures, can survive the transition to a one-world organization. Perhaps it is helpful to remember that humanity has made many complex transitions before; and to achieve stability with large numbers of individuals, man has invented an impressive array of economic, political, and social institutions.

Perhaps the evolution of the United States can help us to imagine the evolution of international cooperation and organization. We did not create a national identity simply by signing up new states to join the Union. With each new state, our inter- and intrastate rules and institutions changed to accommodate the new needs and new opportunities of the expanded organism. Today it would be essentially impossible for New Jersey to declare war on Pennsylvania, for the borders of the two states are so highly transcended politically, economically, and socially that a typical Pennsylvanian could not easily be identified by language or appearance. Furthermore, such a large base of common experience exists that agreements are relatively easily made and honored. But that was not always the case. In creating this unity and stability, the influence of the federal government was probably less important than the catalytic effect of many people working across the borders in common enterprises.

Mankind now requires a new, planet-wide social organization. Technology has caused a vast increase in the range of extant social forms, since old forms do not disappear merely because medical advances or an industrial revolution or fast transportation has produced new ones. But technology has not only increased the range of social forms; it is also forcing their interaction. New forms of communication and transportation have generated new levels of awareness everywhere. No nation can any longer pretend to function in isolation. If any one nation depletes the supply of blue whales, no blue whales remain, even for countries that outlawed their killing. Atomic pollution is pollution for all. Upsetting our protective ozone layer by too many SSTs or by too many aerosol cans would create serious environmental problems everywhere.

In his book *The Meaning of the Twentieth Century,* Kenneth Boulding (1964) divides history into two main periods: precivilization and civilization. The development of agriculture, the domestication of animals, and the development of metallurgy underlie the transition from precivilized to civilized society. Civilized society is characterized by the evolution of great cities and large empires. In Boulding's view, the twentieth century marks the middle period of a second great transition, from civilized to postcivilized society, based on an intensive advance in science and technology, and vastly increased knowledge and knowledge industries. In postcivilized society, nationality separates people less than whether or not they participate in knowledge and technology networks.

Dividing history into different periods helps put into perspective how long social transitions take. Given that we are already well into a second major transition, we also recognize that parts of the world have not yet begun the first transition.

If we are to avoid a future in which isolated and alienated countries continue to do battle based on varying brands of tunnel vision, we need to find ways for a wider range of individuals to begin to work together on our common problems. As more and more people cross and recross national borders, eventually the interactions between different cultures become so complex that they do not yield easily to war, even though conflicts persist. As international networks of problem solvers develop, the dominating influence of any one group — whether they be businessmen, politicians, or generals — will diminish. No single problem-solving group will have a complete view of the world or foolproof, broad-based solutions. But the greater the number of groups and views, the higher our probability of evolving sound solutions.

Those in this country who promote local involvement stress the value of developing directories that can steer people to resources and to other people with common interests. The international need is equally great. Current international directories could be augmented with inventories of people whose skills and experience lie in meeting common needs as well as in the more sophisticated areas of monetary agreements, arms control, or the development of new satellite transmission systems.

Although our languages and our customs vary enormously, our common problems can provide a basis for a common language, even if specific solutions and detailed approaches differ according to custom and tradition.

Violence and Aggression

Some people feel that aggression and violence are basic human drives that must continually be satisfied. Robert Ardrey, for example, espoused such a view in his *African Genesis,* (1961). In reporting on the mysteries of Africa's Olduvai Gorge, Ardrey traces man through the treacherous Pleistocene epoch and concludes that, though we have indeed come a long way, our basic problem is that we are born killers — in fact, that we were armed predators long before we even achieved our modern, enlarged brain. Granting some evidence, which it is for history to judge, let us consider a slight alteration in point of view.

Systems seem to evolve new functions not purely by replacement but also by the inhibition of older functions. The presence of an older function is made apparent if the older function somehow becomes disinhibited. In this sense, the violence and killing that are part of man's heritage can be thought of as modes that are released, or that we regress to, under pressure.

In stressful times, believing in man's inherent violence may well lead to different strategies than believing that violence is the result of tension, stress, and imbalance. The former view would tend to emphasize armaments and "not giving an inch"; the latter to taking slightly more risks in the search for new ways to restore the balance.

Impediments and Dangers

At the same time that we promote increased interaction among diverse nations, we also recognize the dangers of increased knowledge of other cultures and of increased trust. With a greater common base of experience, the rogue, the scoundrel, and the oppressor can more easily identify the weak points of a potential adversary, can assess threats more intelligently, and can have a higher chance of penetration for evil purposes. However, the alternative to the risk is hopelessness. With continually increasing ease of international transportation and communication, widely diverse and powerful cultures are thrust into ever more intense interaction and competition. With properly structured flow and interaction, we can at least hope for the evolution of new methods of problem solving.

To increase interaction is not to achieve anything new but to recognize that new kinds of forces require new forms of interaction. If we are not to rely on war, we must substitute other means. It is true that promoting further interaction will raise new kinds of problems. However, change is already in motion: The muezzin calls the faithful to the mosque with the aid of a 1000-watt amplifier; New Guinea tribesmen wear sun glasses and alarm clocks as status symbols and IUDs (intrauterine devices) as decoration. Multinational corporations are generating change in ways we cannot conceivably predict. The change and the flow cannot be stopped and the world set back to some original state of innocence. What we can do is try to establish interaction that we perceive as constructive and begin to build problem-solving mechanisms. To leave the field solely to exporters of consumables, exploiters of cheap labor, and armies of resource-devouring corporations is not only unwise but also impossible. A person with a gun or a little plastic explosive can say "no"; a government that controls large oil reserves can impose new demands on oil-poor customers; trade wars can be undertaken.

ONE PEACEFUL EXPEDITIONARY FORCE
PER GENERATION

Individuals who desire to be on the move internationally represent an important national resource. We can help those individuals — some of whom might be in a recycling mode looking for new opportunities, some of whom might be interested in plying their current trade in a new context, and some of whom might simply be looking for new experiences — by facilitating that flow.

How many people might eventually be involved in such international efforts? Suppose that one-half of 1 percent of the U.S. population, some 1 million people, were continually abroad for, say, two years each. Then every twenty years (about one generation), 10 million Americans would have had actual living experience in other lands. Interestingly, that is just about what we've had recently through other mechanisms: one American expeditionary force per generation.

As individuals and as a society, we can respond realistically only to that which we comprehend as real, and we find it difficult to grasp the reality of that which we do not experience directly. Facilitating the movement of many citizens internationally could help us all to appreciate the reality of the world outside our borders.

Some of these people who spent time abroad would emerge as leaders and representatives. From their own experiences abroad, they would tend to have a more realistic response to foreign relations, neither overfearful out of ignorance nor blind to dangers. Also, with so many people on the move internationally, it would not be long before our own educational system began to confirm, in a substantive way, that there really are other and different lifestyles across the globe and that these other lifestyles are real and worth knowing.

In the following chapter, we put the idea of international exchange into a broader context: that of international "recycling."

Part Two
RECYCLING AND
EDUCATION

Part One explored the future through a vision of a maturing social marketplace that could help us to cope with our social problems and our information needs.

Part Two explores the future from a more personal perspective. First, it postulates the need for a more flexible relationship between the individual and society—encapsulated here in the notion of a recycling lifestyle. An extended social marketplace would be an important component of a successful recycling mode; and recycling, in turn, would be important to the continual evolution of the social marketplace. Second, it examines certain components of our educational system that seem to need specific emphasis in order to cope with rapid social change.

VII
RECYCLING CAREERS
AND LIFESTYLES

Spaceflight offers a model for life development that is different from the straight-as-an-arrow rifle shot. Because of incomplete knowledge and unanticipated events, it is impossible to aim a spacecraft on exactly the right course in a single step; continual monitoring of the flight and multiple mid-course corrections are absolute necessities. With complex life patterns, multiple midlife corrections for individuals —in place of the traditional three-part life model of education, a fixed career, and retirement—seem equally necessary. In fact, with rapid social change and rapid change in career opportunities, the age-old question "What do you want to be when you grow up?" becomes more and more difficult for young people to answer. Rather than being chastised for "not being able to hold a job," those who respond to this new social need by a generally flexible working career might become the heroes of a more advanced "recycling" society.

This chapter suggests that easier means for individuals to leave a productive phase of their life, enter a phase of exploration, and reenter society in a new productive role—that is, to recycle themselves—would ameliorate many of our major personal and societal problems. Among the means suggested are larger living units in place of the isolated nuclear family; a shift from a single, final retirement to a series of sabbaticals throughout life; lifelong education as a major new service sector; mechanisms of social support; the exploration opportunities offered by an extended social mar-

ketplace; and, to match the rapid change at our national borders, mechanisms for international recycling. A society with a substantial number of its people in a legitimate exploratory mode (rather than unemployment or an outcast mode) would also create a social milieu highly conducive to the evolution of the social marketplace we are considering.

The combination of increased life expectancy and rapid social change has made obsolete our traditional three-part life model of education, career, and retirement. We need a more flexible relationship between the individual and society if we are to adjust easily and successfully to continuously changing social conditions. If one could "recycle" one's life more easily by changing jobs, careers, and even lifestyles in response to social forces or inner propensities, many social problems would be ameliorated. The need for such recycling grows out of several social trends:

- *Unneeded people.* Only a small fraction of our population is needed now to produce our basic physical goods, and we have been unable to find valued roles for people displaced by our highly efficient production system.
- *Obsolescence.* Rapid technological change can cause jobs, careers, and lifestyles to become obsolete rapidly, often adding to the ranks of the "unneeded" people.
- *Dissatisfaction.* Many people are dissatisfied with aspects of our production-oriented and work-driven industrial society. At the same time, no widely accepted alternatives have emerged strongly enough to ease the confusion of those in transition to new lifestyles.
- *Longer life expectancy.* For too many of our people, the patterns established for retirement make old age a punishment instead of a reward. Proposals such as increased social security payments impose even greater burdens on those within the production system and do not solve the psychological problems of the aged in a society that regards them as obsolete and commits them in increasing numbers to institutions.
- *Isolated nuclear family.* The traditional family was an important force toward industrialization as well as a result of it. Each family unit needed to provide for itself a full complement of basic goods, thereby stimulating production. Furthermore, with fewer basic goods made at home or handed down, each breadwinner became tightly locked into the work ethic; no one outside the family could share the load. Now a high divorce rate, a reluctance of young people to enter marriage, and serious experimentation with alternative living arrangements all indicate that the traditional nuclear family is dysfunctional in certain important ways. The isolation of today's family cuts people off from access to support in stress situations and impedes flexible responses to change. The limitations of resources and the finite ability of the biosphere to handle waste are also coming into conflict with the mass duplication of physical goods required by myriad separate living units.

CHANGING PATTERNS IN LIFESTYLES

Although there was always great variety, the dominant lifestyle of the past was built around a relatively large family entity. A family group spanned all ages and lived either in a single dwelling or as close neighbors. Children's lifestyles and employment patterns tended to parallel those of their parents or other close adults. The guiding ethic was work and production and looking forward to rest and old age. We might refer to this lifestyle as *multigenerational* since the basic living unit and working style encompassed several generations.

In our conversion to an industrialized, technological society, we have become more *one-generational*, both in our perception of time and in our modes of thought. Our guiding ethic still takes its cue from ideas of hard work and high productivity, and the educational system is still considered the necessary forerunner to a productive life. However, in the transition from a rural, agrarian society to an urban and suburban one, the size of our living units and their coherence have been significantly reduced. The nuclear family has taken the place of the manor house and the large family farm; similarly, education and retirement have become institutions in themselves, separate from the family. Children no longer follow closely in their parents' footsteps, and lifestyles now tend to follow one-generational rather than multigenerational patterns. In addition, with the high rate of technological change that characterizes the late twentieth century, job opportunities and job forms can change significantly in a single working lifetime. As a result, not only do parent and child often have different lifestyles, but they increasingly choose, or are forced into, different occupations and ways of living several times even within their own productive lives.

The linear pattern of a preparatory phase (education), a productive phase (life work of one kind), and retirement is no longer satisfactory for many people caught up in the current of rapid social change. We are discovering a need for a type of social recycling — the voluntary and productive adaptation of individuals to new careers and new perceptions. We can best describe this mode as *subgenerational* because it requires many readjustments within the lifetime of a single individual.

The needs and opportunities of a society that facilitates recycling will be accompanied by shifts in some fundamental patterns. Figure 8 suggests one such shift — namely, larger living units based not so much on blood relationship as on common interest. Thus, although the isolated nuclear family is not likely to be replaced by the commune, the

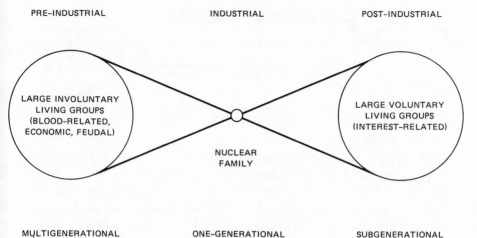

PRE-INDUSTRIAL   INDUSTRIAL   POST-INDUSTRIAL

LARGE INVOLUNTARY LIVING GROUPS (BLOOD-RELATED, ECONOMIC, FEUDAL)

NUCLEAR FAMILY

LARGE VOLUNTARY LIVING GROUPS (INTEREST-RELATED)

MULTIGENERATIONAL   ONE-GENERATIONAL   SUBGENERATIONAL

Figure 8   Change in lifestyle modes.

range of living possibilities will widen. Many will continue to live multi-generationally or one-generationally, but more and more people will live subgenerationally. Future perspective may well show that the isolated nuclear family was an unstable transition form between large living units based primarily on blood relationship and more flexible ones based more on common interests and convenience.

RELAXING OUR BORDERS

Every society is defined by social and economic borders that are important to the definition and functioning of the society and that distinguish the economically productive elements from the outsiders or outcasts of the system. Traditionally, we have defined our "insiders" based on qualities of productivity, a strong work ethic, and raising children to respect the system. We have ignored, neglected, or ostracized our deviants according to the degree of their deviation. However, our guiding ethic is now subject to change, because America's industrialization has been so successful that we are confronted with people without roles and a somewhat shaky work ethic.

Figure 9 is a schematic representation of our society's borders. The area inside the large box represents the economically productive component of American society. Across the top is an internal border (really a system of borders) above which lie the intended and unintended outcasts of society—the financially dependent (poor, unemployed, severely

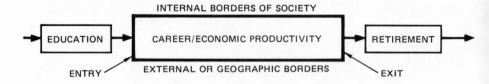

Figure 9 The spatial and temporal borders of our economic system.

handicapped), criminals, the mentally ill, subversives, the drug culture, and "dropouts." The lower external or geographic border distinguishes our nation from other nations. From the perspective of the insider, those living outside the internal borders might be viewed as living in storage institutions such as prisons, hospitals, skid rows, and rehabilitation centers. Even education, retirement, and the military now fall, in large part, into the category of storage institutions.[1]

We can think of the longitudinal borders as guardrails that have kept insiders flowing down the middle, attracted by our particular system of rewarding effort with money, status, and finally retirement. These borders are essentially spatial borders. Figure 9 also defines two temporal borders labeled "entry" and "exit." These borders mark the beginning and end of economic productivity; the educational system precedes entry and the institution of retirement follows an individual's exit from economically productive channels.

ELEMENTS OF DYSFUNCTION

Each of the borders represented in Figure 9 is now dysfunctional in certain ways, a symptom of major social problems. Social dysfunction can be measured in terms of the costs as well as the discomfort that the system generates in both the in and the out groups. When a considerable portion of our resources go toward sustaining and policing borders, it may be time to reassess the elements of the ethic behind our system of borders. The number of people in storage institutions, and the expense of welfare, support, and policing systems give us some measure of the current cost to society of maintaining untenable borders. Let us

[1]William Bevin (1972), describes the "warehousing" system for the elderly:
Increasingly, recourse has been to institutionalization, and increasingly this has meant the nursing home. Today there are in the United States 23,000 nursing homes, with well over a million beds. This is 250 percent more than existed in 1960, and seven new homes open each day . . . . They have been labeled warehouses for the dying. . . .

look first at the elements of dysfunction in our internal border system and then glance at the external or geographic borders.

Borders tend to define a one-way flow, as suggested in Figure 10. It is easy to exit, but it is often difficult to return. A person with a prison record or a record of serious mental disturbance finds it hard to get a job or credit. This may force him onto welfare, increase his chances of returning to crime, or make him sick; he is thereby maintained *outside* social borders. Draft resisters are a recent example of individuals formerly inside societal borders who were subject to exclusion because of this one-way flow.

For the growing numbers of people who want to leave the formal productive channels temporarily for education, job training, or public service, as well as for outsiders who seek new opportunities within the system, this difficulty of reentry presents a major barrier. Facilitating reentry can help both the individual, who is stimulated by new opportunities, and the society, which can benefit from the increased productivity of those reentering.

Another clear symptom of system dysfunction is the growing number of young people who drop out without ever entering the productive phase. These voluntary dropouts, symbolized by the dashed lines in Figure 10, are often fearful of starting down the one-way tunnel and becoming trapped into a life they perceive as unsatisfying and unnecessarily narrow in scope.

On this point, consider a warning by Theodore Roszak, who, in a powerful attack on "technology's essential criminality," hangs our future on a single delicate thread: a limited segment of today's socially

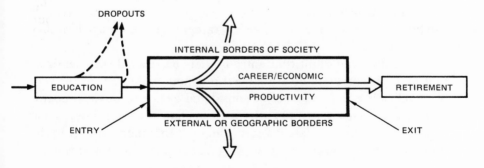

Figure 10   One-way flow through borders.

aware youth. In the introduction to *The Making of a Counter Culture,* he notes:

> They [drop-out youth] are the matrix in which the alternative, but still excessively fragile future is taking shape. Granted that alternative comes dressed in a garish motley, its costume borrowed from many and exotic sources. . .Still it looks to me like all we have to hold against the final consolidation of a technocratic totalitarianism. (1968, p. xiii)

Roszak offers a challenging perspective and an important warning. The job of societal problem solving is not youth's alone, but for its part youth needs real experience in ongoing society in addition to new levels of creativity and awareness and a new sense of exploration. To incorporate all these components, youth must not be driven out of the system. It is essential that society permit certain modes of alienation to exist in order to encourage some segments of its youth to explore new ways. Further, it would be society's as well as the individual's loss if these new experiences could not be incorporated into social experience through legitimate reentry.

In many ways, our educational system has become a type of storage system for youth—for both potential dropouts and future "insiders." Our affluence has not only reduced the need for the services of youth but has made possible longer and longer storage periods in schools. The trend toward specialization further increases the duration of the institutionalization for many students. Sociologist James Coleman (1969) notes that in earlier days society was role-rich but information-poor, with school serving the important function of information enrichment. Our present society is reversed; we now have an overdose of information with fewer opportunities for meaningful roles in using this information. With this reversal, childhood education can no longer be seen primarily as an information-transfer process, and there is a growing need for the educational borders to be relaxed in such a way that schools can be more active forces in the society rather than the storage bins they now in part are.

It is also important that entry borders be relaxed sufficiently so that multiple entry will be available throughout a lifetime. At the very least, schooling can no longer be considered a once-through, preparatory process. With roles and paths likely to change several times in one lifetime, a lifelong education system can play an important part in the transitions. Crowded community colleges on nights and weekends attest to this growing need.

Education must be one of the major institutions of any human re-cycling effort. As a potentially major "service sector," it may also offer relief from problems of unemployment. Perhaps a new answer to our poverty of meaningful social roles will be the use of personnel to provide lifelong education for career, lifestyle, and job transitions.

Solving the problem of resources for lifelong education may also solve another problem of the future. There is deep concern about jobs in a mature technological society in which only a small fraction of the labor force is needed for satisfying basic physical needs. More and more, planners and strategists look toward the "service sector" for filling the employment gap. But there is confusion about exactly what the service sector is: Is it more insurance companies, more hairdressers, more help in filling out income tax forms, more masseuses and masseurs? Perhaps the largest component of the new service sector will be education; and perhaps a new answer to our poverty of meaningful social roles will be the use of personnel to provide lifelong education for career, lifestyle, and job transitions.

RECYCLING

It is often argued that most of us will become superfluous as a smaller and smaller percentage of the work force is needed to produce our required goods and services and that this is sufficient rationale to eliminate the strong work ethic. Some conclude from this argument that, since we are *all* the legitimate beneficiaries of many generations of industrious forefathers, we should simply share the wealth and let those people work who want to, for extra funds or by personal preference. The usual image that underlies this idea of a post-industrial society is that a great share of our time and energy will be available to focus on higher-level individual growth and fulfillment.

On the other hand, we need only look at world history to see that no society has long survived and prospered after it abandoned its com-mitment to an ethic that included serious and sustained work. We are caught, then, between two images — a work ethic that no longer fully serves our needs and a need for greater flexibility. America is in the posi-tion of a landowner who purchased hillside property for future develop-ment, only to discover himself caught between the need to protect his investment and his commitment to new movements to "save the hills." If this landowner is to balance these perceptions, he will need a flexible position between the two. If he has alternative sources of reward and income, he need not protect his investment quite so fiercely and can perhaps find a happy combination of monetary and psychological rewards in using his property for ecologically sound projects that bring adequate gain as well.

Similarly, as we recognize that our fundamental social paradigm is shifting (although we don't yet know how best to guide it), we must keep a firm hand on productivity while allowing, even encouraging, simultaneous experiments in new directions. A recycling lifestyle, with the easier exit and reentry afforded by recycling mechanisms, would be one way to increase the breadth of productive channels open to individuals. This flexibility is critical—it allows people access to different ways to earn rewards and income, so that no one decision need be ruinous.

Relaxing the societal borders we have just described can enable us to recycle our lives more smoothly and productively. Thoreau describes one recycling ritual of an American Indian culture:

> When a town celebrates the busk [the "feast of first fruits"], having previously provided themselves with new clothes, new pots, pans, and other household utensils and furniture, they collect all their worn out clothes and other despicable things, sweep and cleanse their houses, squares, and the whole town, of their filth, which with all the remaining grain and other old provisions they cast together into one common heap, and consume it with fire. After having taken medicine, and fasted for three days, all the fire in the town is extinguished. During this fast they abstain from the gratification of every appetite and passion whatever. A general amnesty is proclaimed; all malefactors may return to their town. On the fourth morning, the high priest, by rubbing dry wood together, produces new fire in the public square, from whence every habitation in the town is supplied with the new and pure flame. (1953, p. 51)

At a symbolic level, this type of ritual can serve as a model of a society programmed for periodic, cooperative cleansing and smooth reentry for those formerly outside the social borders. In a large, pluralistic society such as ours, however, we need a mechanism for recycling according to natural individual rhythms or the exigencies of change. The ability to leave and reenter the mainstream of society in different styles at different times, without stigma, holds part of the solution to some of our major societal problems.

We will need institutions that can help us to develop alternative bases of earning rewards and income so that individuals can change course in response to either social change or personal preference. Such institutions would serve those dissatisfied with their first career choice, those whose work becomes obsolete, as well as voluntary and involuntary dropouts. Figure 11 suggests two such recycling routes: Path 1 illustrates a reentry stage for those wishing to soften the borders of retirement; path 2 is a possible pattern of reentry for those formerly outside our borders—a type of "malefactor route."

Employers, too, must be able to shift rapidly and change personnel smoothly if they are to keep their institutions viable and relevant. Today management is often constrained in such actions because of the unfortunate consequences of dismissal. However, if an employee remains at a job simply because it is difficult to start over, the institution and society lose as well as does the individual. With society geared for greater recycling, individuals and their institutions would both have greater freedom to respond appropriately to change. Although not all of us would—or should—recycle, we would all benefit if the process were a part of the system rather than a precarious personal venture.

A major factor in our learning to control technology and move smoothly into the post-industrial era is our ability to retain youth in the system. Young people need real experience in ongoing society in addition to a climate that permits creativity, awareness, and a sense of exploration, if they are to move out of "storage" and into the mainstream. Such goals will require our society to foster and encourage those segments of youth who want to serve as a vanguard and explore new lifestyles, rather than isolating them outside our borders of acceptability. With easier exit, redirection, and reentry, the one-way tunnel we have depicted will no longer be a threat and a trap to young people, and they will be spared the social pressure to choose the "right course" the first time around. For those who do drop out, the greater ease of reentry or rehabilitation would accrue to society's gain.

Successful reentry presupposes the individual's desire to return, an effective means for accomplishing the return, and acceptance by society. The existence of common machinery for return of both the voluntary dropout and the so-called "malefactor" would not only facilitate role flexibility but would also decrease the stigma associated with rehabilitation. The "outs" and "ins" would meet in the process, further facilitating the integration of both in the society.

Recycling and other forms of rehabilitation are also blocked or opposed when society assigns permanent stigmas. For instance, a person who loses voting rights permanently can never be fully recycled. What

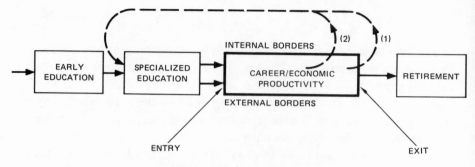

Figure 11   Different recycling modes.

we may need in general is a greater proportion of records that eventually forget. The period prior to forgiveness may be determined by (1) what society believes is a useful detention time necessary to deter others from committing similar crimes, (2) the time necessary for completing certain rehabilitation processes, and (3) the desire to speed the return of as many individuals as possible. The shorter the assigned period to forgiveness, the more rapidly the society drives the recycling process.

Recycling can provide a *natural* flow for members of society and a highly reasonable method of responding to change. It would increase the chance for individuals to track their yearnings in a legitimate sequence of modes and lifestyles, as well as increase the range of opportunities for institutions to respond to change. Besides increasing an individual's freedom to grow and develop, easier recycling would make the recognition of personal discomfort with an existing situation a stimulus for change rather than a source of despair or evasive or destructive action. It is questionable whether a law-and-order treatment of boundary maintenance can have such positive value. On a broader scale, even in economic terms alone, society benefits from any recycling that enables a person—outcast or otherwise—to move into a more productive and satisfying life.

DEVELOPING RECYCLING MECHANISMS

Larger Living Units

Those people who want to move from a productive phase to an exploratory or learning phase may find that the cost of travel, communication, and education requires that they simplify and pare down their lifestyles. They could most certainly benefit from new social bonds that would allow for mutual support and the pooling of resources.

Larger living-learning units for persons in the exploratory phase would take some of the support load from current workers and reduce the usual costs of temporary living quarters. Such living units could take a variety of forms—commune, co-op, boarding house, residence club, artists' colony, or elements of all these. The model provided by medieval universities could be borrowed from if students wished to band together for living and education. (Conventional marriage could survive this forming and reforming process if change and growth in both partners were to become part of marriage rather than a threat to it.)

Finally, larger living units could profitably accommodate a wide spread in ages, providing older people with an opportunity to share their accumulated experience and talent and providing young and old alike with an important perspective and stimulus.

From Retirement to Sabbaticals

Our society provides long periods for exploration, free from work commitments, only at the beginning and end of a working life. Yet retirement, for many, is simply a terminal period of unemployment, marked by extreme loneliness and feelings of uselessness. With our excess labor force, however, we could afford to extend a sabbatical leave to employees in all occupations at any time in life, offering a time for recycling or a temporary period of exploration preceding new employment. In this manner, all who wanted to could step out of their workaday life periodically and perhaps better prepare themselves for a final retirement by varied experience and expansion of interests.

This conversion of routine retirement into a sequence of sabbaticals spread over a lifetime raises important questions of financial support and proper early education to prepare individuals for the needs and opportunities of recycling and nonworking periods.

Societal Support for Recycling

When our society sees the advantage of larger-scale recycling, we will invent ways to finance it. For instance, retraining and continuous education might be supported through vouchers such as those recently considered for childhood education; or one might purchase a new education as one purchases a house—by mortgage. Retirement funds might profitably be altered to include not only "early retirement" but periodic payout as well. There are many potential mechanisms to explore; portable (that is, transferable) pensions and seniority are examples of ideas currently being promoted to facilitate this form of movement.

We might also establish a broader set of social service opportunities, in which the military is just one form of service. A limited period of social service at public expense, with individuals choosing when to serve their term, would encourage greater participation of the sort we discussed in Chapter I. A governmentally supported, voluntary social service (like VISTA) would in many ways take on the character of an internal Peace Corps. Voluntary social service might also be an approved mode for recycling later in life.

Relation to the Social Marketplace

Successful recycling not only requires psychological and financial support and social approval, but individuals must be able to explore easily "what is going on in society." If an individual closes out one career because it is no longer viable or of interest in a rapidly changing society, what new and interesting opportunities are on the horizon?

A social market system that includes the kinds of institutions discussed in Part One—an array of specialized centers, distribution systems, and ways for multisector groups to share exploratory experiences —would offer many individuals the opportunity for productive exploration. The other side of the coin is that individuals in a recycling mode would be important candidates as resource assistants or for temporary jobs, leading to more permanent positions for some in many of these new opportunities.

In short, an expanded social marketplace that specializes in social exploration could profit from individuals who are themselves in an exploratory mode. Individuals who may be leaving a highly operational phase of their life to explore new opportunities would, in fact, find the process extremely frustrating without such opportunity. Thus, recycling and an extended social marketplace would seem to serve highly complementary needs.

INTERNATIONAL RECYCLING

Any satisfactory approach to comprehensive recycling must account also for the relaxation of the boundaries between us and the rest of the world. Problems of armaments, food, resources, and pollution all require that we eventually transcend our geographic boundaries and achieve meaningful international agreement and cooperative action.

Underdeveloped nations still have immense problems in meeting their basic needs. Their wants are both a problem for our own security and an opportunity for our cooperation. Some question whether we should aim at artificially reducing automation and productivity simply to make the work go around, when other parts of the world are crying for increased production to meet minimal necessities; others suggest that we continue the growth of technology but redirect its course. Part of the latter approach might profitably include a kind of international recycling, with enormous potential for serving the interests of both individuals and nations.

Individuals who are looking for new career or lifestyle opportunities, are interested in plying their current trade in a new context, or are simply looking for new experiences in other lands represent an important national and international resource. Facilitating the movement of many citizens internationally could help us all to incorporate the world outside our borders into our reality, and to reduce the uneasiness that seems to arise from our inability to accept or understand what we do not experience directly. As noted in Chapter VI, if one-half of 1 percent of the present United States population, some 1 million people, are abroad at some sort of international center or involved in employee interchanges, recycling episodes, or someday even international traveling shows, for an average of two years, then every twenty years 10 million Americans would have experienced actual living in other lands. Some of these people would emerge as leaders and representatives, or new-age brokers — realistic builders of healthy foreign relations, neither fearful out of ignorance nor blind to dangers. Almost everyone would benefit in some way.

At the moment, only incipient international demand mechanisms exist for recycling of individuals, except at the level of cheap labor. Nonetheless, over time a steady flow could be established in which families or individuals could cross the borders for a period of life abroad. If this possibility could be made real, increasing numbers of individuals would undoubtedly perceive as socially important and personally satisfying the opportunity to help fill large unmet needs in other countries and to build bridges among diverse cultures.

Those who doubt that we can afford large numbers of people spending periods abroad should recall how we currently address the problem of unneeded people — shorter work days and work weeks, longer vacations, and earlier retirement, with all the additional problems that these attempted solutions create; that is, large numbers of people are already being cast out of the productive system, either earlier in life or for longer temporary periods.

Even if national disparities prevent us from moving too rapidly in developing direct people-to-people exchange, it seems imperative at least to sustain and slowly expand the kinds of efforts represented by the Peace Corps and such private organizations as the International Voluntary Services, which promote people-to-people exchange and problem solving at the basic skills level. Legitimacy of return is critical, however, as are international agreements on right to work and reduced restrictions. Our educational system and media can play an important role in helping to define the possibilities and mechanisms for this ultimate outgrowth of increased personal recycling.

VIII

EDUCATING FOR CHANGE

Basing the exploration of new social patterns and relationships as broadly as possible among the whole population means developing a more exploratory educational process and developing, in particular, greater experience with both the operational and the exploratory aspects of living and problem solving.

Each of the ideas discussed in this chapter—bringing society back into education, students teaching students, and developing a stronger link to the social curriculum—would help to create new roles for youth, develop an exploratory environment, minimize the fear of failure, lessen the demands now made on teachers, and reduce the cost of education.

To the extent that society is brought back into education and education back into society, the educational system can play a focal role in tracking and guiding social change, with better integration and coordination among the efforts of citizens of all ages.

A movie camera taking one picture every 15,000 years of the Earth's 5-billion-year history would generate a movie strip requiring more than eight hours of viewing, with the million or so years that constitute the Age of Man filling only the last few seconds of the movie. If the last picture had been shot some 10,000 years ago, when man first learned about agriculture and domesticating animals, the next picture would not be due for another 5,000 years. But much has happened in that relatively short time. Ten thousand years ago, the population of the earth is estimated to have been some 10 million people, and growing at less than 1,000 persons per year up to that time. The current population is about 4 billion people, and growing at the rate of almost 80 million per year. The world is filling up rapidly! Population growth, combined with explosive advances in communication, transportation, and weapon systems in a relatively short time, is rapidly forcing the many diverse cultures into tense interaction and competition. Short-term parochial views cannot stand long against the onslaught. Formal education has a critical role in helping individuals cope with a future in which changes may be more concentrated than ever.

We may look back with nostalgia to a simpler time when education was mainly a family affair, but formal education is needed for developing a properly exploratory American society during our third century. To minimize our blindness to patterns, to accommodate to the needs of a recycling society, to master the social curriculum, to feel comfortable with increased worldwide interaction will require that children have a rich and highly organized training, a task that is impossible for the individual family to accomplish alone. With a slight alteration in utilization of media-knowledge resources, our highly organized educational system can help educate children to live more comfortably and more effectively in a rapidly integrating world.

Loren Eiseley refers to an evolutionary "foetalization" process, by which he means the retention into adult life of bodily characteristics that at some earlier stage of evolution were merely infantile. He notes that man has evolved the most helpless childhood of any of the animals. The emergent creature is not whole until, as Eiseley says,

> . . . the dreams of the group, the social constellation amidst which his own orbit was cast, had been implanted in the waiting, receptive substance of his brain. (1946, p. 121)

It is during this extended process of childhood that our brain — which trebles in size following birth — is infused with the patterns of society. The child is exposed to the social patterns that develop in him the neural patterns which tend to make him an imitator. However, there is immense room for variation, and it is in this freedom that we can trace the processes of rapid change and adaptation.

Recall the old story of the meteorologist, engineer, physicist, and salesman who were each given a barometer accurate enough to measure the height of a particular church steeple. The meteorologist took a reading at the ground, another at the top of the steeple, and from his pressure charts found the answer. The engineer climbed to the top of the steeple, lowered his barometer on a long rope, and paced off the rope. The physicist dropped his barometer from the top of the steeple and timed its fall with a stopwatch. The salesman asked the church sexton the height of the steeple, and gave him the barometer as a present.

Children can learn to understand and appreciate that there really are validly different ways to do things and that one person's tool is not necessarily another's. But to travel comfortably in a world of complexity and interactive problems takes a great deal of training and experience. Yet we can learn to communicate effectively with each other, become involved, discuss complex matters, consider unclear questions with even less clear answers, have an outlet for our hidden thoughts, and understand another person's concepts and images. To use our magnificent mental facilities primarily for the storing of predigested facts, to parrot simple answers, to concentrate only on grammar instead of meaning will not help our children to develop the breadth of guiding images that will be necessary for living successfully in our third century.

THREE NEEDS

Coping successfully with complex and often rapidly changing sets of national and international issues will require that third-century America be a highly exploratory society. To train effective explorers, we must become organized to:

- Let children gain experience in the exploratory as well as the operational modes of problem solving (in the sense of Chapter I).
- Find real roles for youth both inside and outside the schoolroom; for this it is necessary to break down the isolation between the educational system and society (the real world outside school).

- Avoid conditioning a fear of failure, a conditioning that derives in part from insufficient exploratory experience and a lack of real roles.

To meet the challenge, educational institutions will need to develop new roles that allow for flexibility and more "real-world" learning. These new roles will require some alteration in educational perspective, new kinds of linkages to the community, and better use of all our knowledge resources.

DEVELOPING A NEW EDUCATIONAL PERSPECTIVE

In his book *How Children Fail*, John Holt notes that

. . . We adults destroy most of the intellectual and creative capacity of children by . . . making them afraid, afraid of not doing what other people want, of not pleasing, of making mistakes, of failing, of being *wrong*. Thus we make them afraid to gamble, afraid to experiment, afraid to try the difficult and unknown. (1964, p. 167)

R. D. Laing offers an even more devastating evaluation when he suggests that fear of failure is a norm of our society and that our alienation is partly conditioned by our schools. In his view, the continual experience of failure that we offer children in school forces

. . . every man reared in our culture, over and over again, night in, night out, even at the pinnacle of success, to dream not of success, but of failure. In school the external nightmare is internalized for life. (1967, p. 71)

Whereas a conditioned fear of failure may be precisely what our evolving industrial society required for rapid development in the past, a primary function of our third-century educational system must be to provide an environment in which children can learn in an atmosphere of constructive feedback and freedom. Such an atmosphere should encourage ongoing exploration in addition to skill acquisition so that learners can better prepare for the roles they will be called on to play in an extended national and international social marketplace.

Schools are presently weak in the exploratory aspects of learning. They must encourage students to experiment more, much as a tennis player must rally between serious games. Rallying is a time for relaxed experimentation and perfecting of techniques that can then be tested in serious games. These, in turn, point up deficiencies and define the needs of subsequent practice sessions. Each type of play feeds into the other in a steady learning process, like the exploration-operation cycles of Figure 3.

So, too, in life, an individual must be able to "rally" as well as to play seriously—to function in an exploratory mode as well as in an operational mode. It is a matter of delicate balance: To have a sense of security, a person adheres to the rules and develops strategies accordingly; but to grow and to understand, he or she experiments with new techniques, responses, ideas, and syntheses.

Just as researchers seek free "rallying" time in which to think way-out thoughts, explore the field, or make false starts, so do students need free time in which to explore beyond rote learning. Without the safety of free time, exploration tends to stop. This is the problem with high-pressure school, high-pressure jobs, and high-pressure living: Continual serious playing prevents new growth. Safety to explore is what our educational system must and can supply, for a classroom based on real-world models is *the* place to explore.

Fear of failure is a hindrance to exploratory problem solving, but so is the pretense that failure can be abolished. If a pilot's flight simulator gives him confidence but not the full set of skills, he will be a danger to us all. Similarly, measurement of skill acquisition is necessary if we are to have competent third-century citizens, but such performance criteria should be limited to the operational skills half of education. No one could "fail" in exploration any more than Columbus failed by finding America rather than a new route to India.

Another characteristic of our schools has been our emphasis on a teaching rather than a learning environment. Infants, for example, learn their native language at their own pace and with full emotional involvement. We can call this a learning environment because the "student" is free to select the knowledge he requires when he needs it and finds ready help in expanding in the direction his intellectual curiosity takes him. A foreign language is usually taught by an entirely different process, however; the student learns by translation. When he learns the word for "cookie," for instance, he learns the word alone and not the associations with smells, tastes, love, and mother that he would receive as he learned in his native tongue. His learning is bare and abstract and dependent on a teacher who controls the "right" answers.

Transforming our current teaching environments to learning environments goes hand-in-hand with the encouragement of more exploration in education. In a learning environment, a student is judged by how well he or she masters a skill or synthesizes a body of knowledge; in a teaching environment, the measure is how well the student adopts and mimics the teacher's method. This difference emphasizes one of the difficulties in creating a learning environment; it is easy to judge how well students can reproduce what their teacher has told them, but it requires a highly experienced or talented teacher to judge how well a student is exploring mathematics, or physics, or history.

Finally, in a highly specialized, affluent society youth have very little opportunity to give to others. Affluence not only reduces the need for their services but enables us to isolate them for long periods. Specialization makes it difficult even to invent useful jobs for them and keeps increasing the duration of the institutionalization, the time required to learn to become "useful." But today's youth is striving for involvement and purpose instead of passive isolation. Society may be able to benefit from this urge because it may, in fact, be easier to give as an adult if one has the opportunity to give as a child. Perhaps, too, it is easier to teach, solve problems, interact, explore, meditate, or introspect as an adult if one has learned how as a child. And it may even be easier to analyze, learn, love, or be aware as an adult if one has had the experience as a child.

We must find real and useful roles for the vigor and the vision of youth, but development of an informed as well as aroused youth is a demanding process requiring great commitment. One step is to let children get more involved with their own education.

MECHANISMS FOR EDUCATIONAL CHANGE

Three opportunities for shifting educational perspective are especially appealing: increasing community involvement in the educational process, a program of students teaching students, and coupling schools more closely to the social curriculum. Each of these would improve teaching, make school a more vital, exciting, and "relevant" place, and help to develop the natural exploratory urge of students.

Bringing the Real World Back into Education

George Leonard offers the following example of an ideal learning situation:

> The automobile makes a perfect teacher. It is a highly interactive learning environment, providing quick feedback for the student driver's every ac-

tion. Anything that can be verbalized by an instructor about this process is trivial compared with what the car in motion tells the learner. The interaction between environment (car in motion) and the learner is frequent, intense and often novel. The learner's behavior is changed during the process. And, at best, learning to drive is ecstatic. (Ask any sixteen-year-old.) Little wonder, then, that practically every human on the planet can become in this respect — when we stand back and apprehend the miracle for what it is — a superman. (1968, p. 38)

Simulation is an old form of training. Red Cross "new father" classes use baby dolls that won't bleed if pricked with a diaper pin or bruise if they are dropped. Airline pilots learn to fly giant jets in a simulator. The pilots learn at their own pace in a completely safe, low-cost environment before entering the real world of crowded airspace, unfamiliar runways, and bad weather.

An educational system is essentially a giant simulation system in which children can be trained in a relatively safe environment to assume the controls in real life. Until recently, however, our schools often simulated an unreal world: Their physical, social, and moral outlook was generally white Anglo-Saxon whereas the media and city streets showed otherwise; they still taught the glories of past victories whereas the TV news showed the realities of the Vietnam War. Schools emphasized simplistic right–wrong answers, whereas the real world presented many complex questions with no simple answers. Reality is more than bad news, however; the real world values high-level skills and rewards the ability to think, create, respond, and remain balanced. A school system must bring students progressively more in touch with this reality, just as in flight simulators pilots are brought step-by-step into contact with all the controls.

In a simulator, one can permit even dangerous, wicked, and foolish ideas to be expressed. For example, we go to see *Macbeth* and we see political assassination used to advance ambition. We can experience the feelings and effects, but we all know that the actor who plays the king goes home after the performance, not to a mortuary. Permitting a pilot to see and feel what happens if he does something dangerous or foolish in a simulator is a safe way of facing him with the consequences. Schools, too, can tolerate a wide range of such exploratory "foolishness."

A close connection between society and education seems important to a good simulation environment. We need doctors, engineers, mechanics, businesspeople, managers, and politicians with an expanded awareness; and we need young people with both a new consciousness and mastery of the skills basic to society. As was the case in an earlier America, young people should be able to interact and work with the practitioners of these skills earlier in their lives — either through meeting them on their operational home ground or through schoolroom involvement of a variety of specialists.

Even in the lower grades, mechanics, carpenters, musicians, artists, engineers, doctors, psychologists, and others could supplement the work of the full-time teachers, both in transferring specific skills and in encouraging fruitful exploration. A lawyer, for example, could take on an elementary or high school class for an extended time, discussing in some depth such broad questions as: What is law? Where does it come from? Why do we have new laws? Such classroom involvement would go beyond ritualistic career-day visits by opening up long-term inquiry and providing a context for simulation of real-world decision making.

At the same time, the process can help visiting specialists rethink their own axioms and those of their professions. Specialists pass through their extensive training so slowly that they continually adapt unconsciously to each new level, losing sight of the enormous depth of their developed concept structures. Exposure to children passing through earlier stages of concept development can reacquaint specialists with long-forgotten basic assumptions of their fields and feed into their own exploration and decision-making processes in constructive ways.

Students Teaching Students

Teachers currently learn many of their skills as adults through short-term specialized training and then enter the classroom trained as one-way dispensers of information. The typical student-teacher relationship is illustrated by the solid lines in Figure 12. But current experiments in "free universities" and "alternative schools" indicate a deep urge and need on the part of students and their parents to give something personal as well as to passively take in information from accredited authorities. Free universities might not appear so revolutionary to us, however, if we had a more distributed and more continuous process of acquiring learning/teaching skills in our existing educational institutions. As suggested by the dotted lines in Figure 12, we might consider a learning environment in which students operate simultaneously as students and teachers. In such a configuration, teaching could be shared by both adults and children: fifth graders

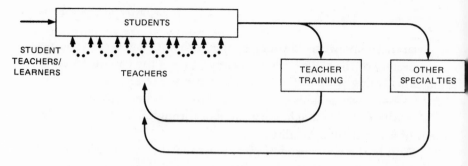

Figure 12   Students teaching students—a continuous system of teaching/
learning.

spending time teaching fourth graders, tenth graders teaching ninth
and eighth graders, college juniors teaching high school seniors, and so
on.

This continuous teaching–learning process could provide a number of important advantages. Helping someone younger while being
helped by someone older can help students develop an affirming sense
of where they have been as well as where they are going. Also, because
peers close in age and development can speak with each other more easily than with teachers, and in some ways understand each other better,
this form of student-to-student interaction might aid in uncovering and
solving personal and classroom problems, as well as facilitate learning.

Another advantage is that anything learned early in life — a language, a sport, an art, a habit — tends to persist. Those who spend a
significant portion of their own developmental period as "teachers" are
likely to acquire a good understanding of the techniques of teaching
and the essential empathy with the learner. Nearly all of us use teaching
skills at some point in coping with our social roles — in bringing up
children, in training subordinates or replacements in a job, in any kind
of supervisory role, or volunteer work.

Perhaps most important of all is that teaching is an important
route to learning. Gartner, Kohler, and Riessman, in their book *Children Teach Children,* note that

> . . . . [L]earning through teaching works for a great variety of reasons, both
> cognitive and emotional. For the tutor, it provides feelings of competency
> and increased self-esteem, develops responsibility and maturity, and may
> even help overcome shyness . . . . [T]he cooperative experience with a peer
> or with a younger child offers an important social experience in contrast to
> the competitive context in which learning generally takes place in our
> society . . . . For the teacher, learning through teaching provides a change
> of pace, is an efficient way to cover material . . . . For the school, the learn-

ing atmosphere is opened up, the school program is derigidified, and more pluralistic forms of learning take place. (1971, pp. 135-136)

Opportunities to try different roles and to interact with individuals on another level are important means of exploring and developing the new images and levels of awareness that our third century will demand. Greater interaction could instill a sense of vital community that could carry through later participation in some of the learning and exploring centers we have discussed. As much as anything, extensive student teaching would offer young people a meaningful social role and a chance to give something significant of themselves as they learn.

Education and the Social Curriculum

Young people are raised in an atmosphere of intense social problems, yet they have minimal, if any, interaction with such social actors as researchers, planners, or decision makers, who seem to affect change. Like their parents, most are isolated from the action. To bridge the gap requires linking the social and academic curricula so as to bring the social actors into closer contact with the schools.

An extended social marketplace would help in several ways. Such things as new regional and local centers and the traveling shows discussed earlier would provide means by which schools could become involved more effectively with social and knowledge goods and services and interact more effectively with social actors. New student internship experiences in the institutions would provide rich and important roles for a great number of young people. With the importance of rapid and continuous feedback to the learner in a simulation environment, local and regional centers would also be in a position to provide schools with invaluable media and knowledge resources of high quality, as well as to coordinate specialist involvement in the schools.

IN CONCLUSION

As technology continues to expand, there will be more and more ways in which children can experiment and rebel. How will parents react when, instead of turning to drugs, youngsters turn to deep freezing for future awakening, or, say, to heart replacement? Surely, some technologist will postulate that a mechanical heart provides greater vitality and a more virile life, or that the real heart releases carcinogenic agents. Prognostication of details is irrelevant, for the potential is clear; what is more relevant is to question how to live with all of these possibilities.

It is important to distinguish exploration and experimentation from rebellion. When rebellion becomes a more or less full-time process, it is a rigid, compulsive mode of life and is fundamentally different from the experimental approach. Experimentation demands rational thought about the material and media involved; full-time rebellion short circuits reason and replaces response with compulsive reaction. Rationally motivated experimentation in a basically healthy environment would be unlikely to lead to massive or serious damage, except in the presence of ignorance. With rebellious or highly frustrated motivation, on the other hand, damage is easily done. Destruction of property and person—self or other—may be the only remedy for emptiness, rejection, or feeling ineffectual. Destruction is a way to prove that one exists.

But having a real role in society is a more beneficial way to prove one's existence. With better access to people, facilities, information, and social action, schools could offer students the kind of organized experience necessary to develop the sense of involvement, trust, insight, reponsibility, and reality that will be necessary for living with complex, rapid change while exploring and enjoying America's third century.

EPILOG

Over the years we have accumulated an impressive range of
scientific knowledge and technical skills. Astronomers have described
our solar system, millions of other galaxies, black holes, neutron stars,
quasars, and concepts deduced from light emitted billions of years ago.
Physicists have taken us from temperatures near absolute zero to
nuclear fusion and earthly temperatures exceeding those of the sun.
Functional systems of integrated electronics are being put on surfaces
the size of a pinhead. Electron microscopes not only let us see such circuits but help us build them. Laser light is giving us flashlights to illuminate the moon. Yesterday's fantasy has yielded to today's reality,
and science fiction writers can hardly keep ahead of real events as we
send rockets to the planets, synthesize organic molecules, and initiate
life in test tubes.

At the same time, the "war to end all wars" was merely a prelude to
increasingly terrifying wars, weapons, and risks that result from the ever
more intense interaction and competition among diverse ideologies,
traditions, and cultures. Yet the interaction among nations is not all
random motion. Technology and the continually increasing relatedness
that it fosters force us ever closer to a planetary consciousness.

Optimism in the search for new national and international order
rests in part on the ability of youth and adults to learn to accommodate to
each other. Generally speaking, adults are more masterful at imple-

menting remedial solutions, whereas young people exercise greater freedom in exploring new ways to approach and promote things as they might be. We need the combination of both. Large design changes cannot be made in a single step; *natural* solutions must evolve as a continual blend of what we are and what we can be.

Optimism can also derive from our recognition that rebellion is not something new under the sun but a signal of societal stress and the need for change:

> A youth approached me. He was bearded; his clothes were dirty; he wore a student's cloak and he looked a typical New Cynic of the sort I deplore. I have recently written at considerable length about these vagabonds. In the last few years the philosophy of Crates and Zeno has been taken over by idlers who, though they have no interest in philosophy, deliberately imitate the Cynics in such externals as not cutting their hair or beards, carrying sticks and wallets, and begging. But where the original Cynics despised wealth, sought virtue, questioned all things in order to find what was true, these imitators mock all things, including the true, using the mask of philosophy to disguise license and irresponsibility. Nowadays, any young man who does not choose to study or to work grows a beard, insults the gods, and calls himself Cynic. (From the Emperor Julian, 1969, p. 331)

Thus, our social order emerges today, as it did in the fourth century A.D., from the continual flow between the constraining walls of radicalism and conservatism. Those who, regardless of age, perceive the need for drastic, fundamental change and those who perceive the need to keep intact the current images and traditional values together define the flow. Caution in departure from established ways is not without reason when one perceives that life itself is on the brink and that even a small error may be disastrous. On the other hand, rebellion and a search for new ways need not be treason.

With the anxiety of living in what could conceivably be the terminal phase of a highly productive industrial era, many make a strong plea for soul over reason, arguing that it is human intellect run wild that has brought us to our current imbalance. Whereas this call to the soul may help rebalance our weighty think-tank approach to problem solving, what we need even more is a mode of problem solving that couples individual and societal needs in a new way. More isolated analyses, and even new types of multidisciplinary or broad-based research centers that remain essentially isolated from the people, will not see us through, nor will uninformed dependence on intuition, heart, or soul. We desperately require both processes—analysis and intuition; finding solutions requires that we create new ideas in an exploratory atmosphere, but implementation requires also that we be able to feel our way in practice and reasoned trial and error.

Our society is so vast and we are experiencing such bewildering change that a sense of isolation and gloom easily grips us. Our government has become so cumbersome and centralized that it seems in many ways more and more unresponsive. At the same time, we are continually exhorted to become more involved. In this book, I have argued that solving our major problems and increasing our individual involvement will require the evolution of a greatly extended decentralized marketplace for social and knowledge goods and services.

This extended marketplace will provide a means of pooling the views of young and old, technologists and lay people, soul and reason — those who seek fundamental change and a new order of justice and those who seek to preserve the status quo. Without mechanisms to focus these disparate energies, each group will go its own frustrated way, seeking out skirmishes and every possibility for attack and advantage. With an organized marketplace, we create a positive foundation for ongoing, long-term sharing of risks, perceptions, and problem-solving processes.

With our American genius for experimenting and our deep craving for and experience with freedom, we perhaps uniquely contain the necessary ingredients for leading the way to a new world, just as we did 200 years ago. Now that we have learned how to meet our basic physical needs, and even how to surfeit ourselves with more physical goods and paraphernalia than we can ever use, it is time to examine our new needs and look for new opportunities. Building an extended social marketplace presents real challenges and opportunities. We will not acquire our new social mechanisms in a single step; they will evolve out of our present know-how, our entrepreneurial and technological talents, our people, and our large and small businesses and institutions. With our third century upon us, the challenge will be difficult to ignore!

REFERENCES

American Academy of Arts and Sciences, *Bulletin of the Academy of Arts and Sciences*, XXV, 6, March 1972.

Ardrey, R. *African genesis*. New York: Delta Publishing Co., 1961.

Bell, D. Welcome to the post-industrial society, *Physics Today*, February 1976, 46–49.

Bevin, W. Editorial, *Science*, September 8, 1972.

Boulding, K. E. *The meaning of the twentieth century*. New York: Harper and Row, 1964.

Coleman, J. S., Education in the age of computers and mass communication. Presented at the lecture series, *Computers, Communications, and the Public Interest*, Johns Hopkins University and the Brookings Institute, December 11, 1969.

Cornuelle, R. C. *Reclaiming the American dream*. New York: Random House, 1965.

de Tocqueville, A. *Democracy in America*. London: Oxford University Press, 1965.

Eiseley, L. *The immense journey*. New York: Random House, 1946.

Emperor Julian. Memoirs. From fourth century A.D., reprinted in *Perspectives in Biology and Medicine*. Chicago: University of Chicago Press, 12, 3, Spring 1969, 331.

Gartner A., Kohler, M., & Riessman, F. *Children teach children: Learning by teaching*. New York: Harper and Row, 1971,

Gould, J. E. *The Chautauqua movement: An episode in the continuing American revolution*. Albany: State University of New York Press, 1961.

Harrison, H. P. *Culture under canvas: The story of tent Chautauqua*. New York: Hastings House, 1958.

Holt, J. *How children fail*. New York: Dell Publishing Co., 1964.

Laing, R. D. *The politics of experience*. New York: Pantheon Press, 1967.

Leonard, G. *Education and ecstasy*. New York: Delta Publishing Co., 1968.

Linvill, W. Technology and the needs of man, *Stanford Today*, Summer 1970, 2–14.

National Academy of Sciences. Ferrocement: Applications in developing countries. Advisory Committee on Technological Innovation, Office of Foreign Secretary, 1973.

Overstreet, H. A. *The mature mind.* New York: W. W. Norton and Co., 1949.

Roszak, T. *The Making of a Counter Culture.* New York: Doubleday and Co. Inc., 1968.

Schumacher, E. F. *Small is beautiful: Economics as if people mattered.* New York: Harper and Row, 1973.

Solo, R. A. *Economic organizations and social systems.* New York: Bobbs-Merrill Co., Inc., 1967.

Szilard, L. *The voice of the dolphins.* New York: Simon and Schuster, 1961.

Taber, R. *The war of the flea.* New York: Citadel Press, 1970.

Thoreau, H. D. *Walden.* Signet Classics. New York: New American Library of World Literature, Inc., 1953.

Wright, Q. *A study of war.* Chicago: University of Chicago Press, 1964 ed.

AUTHOR INDEX

Page numbers in *italics* indicate where complete references are listed.

SUBJECT INDEX

DATE DUE

APR 0 4 2003			

GAYLORD